"Mike has been a friend of mine ~~...~~ parts fun, wise, and kind. He says what he believes, and he believes what he says. This book is full to the brim with words from a voice I trust, because Mike lives out the gospel message without pretense and with tremendous vulnerability."

—Bob Goff, author of *New York Times* bestsellers
Love Does and *Everybody, Always*

"Who is waiting for you when the road rises up and smacks you in the face, when life sneaks up and hits you from behind and knocks you to your knees? Mike Donehey realized that it was from these positions he was in the best place to reach out for God's hand and rise up. From accidents and intentions, decadence to ascension, his life and God's will found a place called home."

—Ken Mansfield, author, producer, and former
US manager of the Beatles' Apple Records

"Some books are fun to read while others just hit home, but my friend Mike Donehey has a way of doing both here. He is brilliant with words; his storytelling makes you laugh out loud; and yet—with all humility—in every chapter he blindsides you with truth that spins you right into freedom. When you have all of this written by someone with the highest values and character, you end up with a resource God uses in your life. This is a must-read."

—Chuck Bomar, pastor of Colossae Church and author
of *Better Off Without Jesus* and *Serving Local Schools*

"At times in our friendship, God has used Mike to tell me exactly what I need to hear at just the right moment. I believe many will feel that Mike has done the same for them after reading *Finding God's Life for My Will*. Reading Mike's words is like getting a new eyeglass prescription. You'll see Jesus and life with new clarity, and the result will be joy, freedom, and peace. This is a great read for anyone looking to take a next step with Jesus while laughing along the way."

—TIMOTHY ATEEK, executive director of Breakaway Ministries

"Challenging, captivating, and convicting. In *Finding God's Life for My Will*, Mike not only offers a refreshing perspective, but he also gives us the wisdom we need to really live the life we were always made for!"

—JORDAN LEE DOOLEY, author of *Own Your Everyday* and host of the *SHE* podcast

"It was a little intense, especially the car-crash part. It's awesome. It's amazing. It's wonderful. It's just a book you can read when you're feeling down. It inspires you to help your feelings courage up so you're feeling happy and have a great new start for the day."

—EISLEY DONEHEY, age nine

"It's very, like, calming, you know? It's very peaceful, you know . . . like . . . it's very good, and it has lots of pages, and I bet you would want to read it."

—NORA DONEHEY, age eight

Finding God's LIFE for My Will

HIS PRESENCE IS THE PLAN

MIKE DONEHEY

WATERBROOK

FINDING GOD'S LIFE FOR MY WILL

Italics in Scripture quotations reflect the author's added emphasis.

Details in some anecdotes and stories have been changed to protect the identities of the persons involved.

Trade Paperback ISBN 978-0-525-65281-6
eBook ISBN 978-0-525-65282-3

Cover design by Kristopher K. Orr; cover image by Jeremy Cowart

Published in the United States by WaterBrook, an imprint of Random House, a division of Penguin Random House LLC.

WATERBROOK® and its deer colophon are registered trademarks of Penguin Random House LLC.

The Cataloging-in-Publication Data is on file with the Library of Congress.

Printed in the United States of America
2019—First Edition

10 9 8 7 6 5 4 3 2 1

SPECIAL SALES
Most WaterBrook books are available at special quantity discounts when purchased in bulk by corporations, organizations, and special-interest groups. Custom imprinting or excerpting can also be done to fit special needs. For information, please email special marketscms@penguinrandomhouse.com or call 1-800-603-7051.

To Kelly,
I love you more.
Giant Squid.

Contents

If This Book Were to Have an Introduction, This Would Be It

The prophet Isaiah says, "Your ears shall hear a word behind you, saying, 'This is the way, walk in it,' when you turn to the right or when you turn to the left" (30:21).

That's nice, but could it really be so simple? To hear the voice of God and to follow where it leads? Isn't that what we're all after? Who wouldn't turn if they heard God's voice over their shoulder? Imagine the Almighty echoing down the halls of your mind like a high school loudspeaker. If we heard God talking, of course we'd respond. The problem is we seldom know whose voice it is we're hearing. It doesn't seem like there's ever just one, does it? Our hearts speak. Our minds speak. Regret screams. Old shame shouts. Our bodies groan. The Spirit whispers. The Devil plays our strings. In the midst of all the noise, how can we possibly know if it's the voice of the Divine we're following or just our own desires?

The New Living Translation renders this verse in Isaiah as "You will hear a voice *right* behind you." This helps immensely. I love the image. What if rather than trying to send calls on a long-range radio, God is hailing us on a walkie-talkie? What if He is perfectly content with the static when we wander too far from His side? What if we were never meant to know the whole plan? Would we be able to take the one step in front of us while trusting He'll speak to the present silence for the next? What if God doesn't want to give us answers because He wants to give us His presence?

I want to be done with overcomplicating things. I want to live this life with more than a ten-year plan. I've tried those and they never work. At least not the way I drew them up. It seems like most of the plans I've made are really just attempts to avoid having to listen and wait for God to come through. I want to be done with that.

I heard a story once of a man who traveled to India to have Mother Teresa pray that he would discover God's plan for his life. She said no. He insisted. She responded flatly, "No, I will not do that. . . . I will pray that you trust God."[1]

I love Mother Teresa's response, and I guess I hate it at the same time. As much as I want to say I trust God, I'd rather feel sure and competent about my future. But that's just it. No one knows the future. And if faith and trust are God's true goals for our lives, then it would make sense He'd have to keep us in the dark on some things in order to cultivate other things inside us.

You have to have some fear before you can take courage. Uncertainty precedes faith, and doubt must take hold before we can exude trust. Trust is what grows in our hearts when we give our doubts over to the love of God. I guess you could call trust the ability to hear God singing Cyndi Lauper's "Time After Time" over your life:

If you fall, I will catch you, I'll be waiting
Time after time[2]

Trust is believing your future is wrapped in the love of God, and if that's the case, then we can trust-fall into wherever God leads. I want to hear His melody over me so loud that all other voices learn their proper harmony to His song. But that takes practice. It takes leaning in every second of every day. Each time we feel He's speaking and we willingly turn away, His voice grows a little fainter against the volume of our well-composed plans. I want to grow in my ability to hear His voice, and I want you to hear Him too. And not just a voice that's always guiding you but a voice that's always changing you. I'm done with anything less.

So this is my story. I'll share how I gave up begging to know God's will and began to ask His life to come and change my will. This is my journey of trying to stop blackmailing God into giving me His secret plan and instead start letting Him change my secret plans. I've come to believe God is much less interested in what we do with our lives and much more concerned with how and why we live our lives. Or perhaps I should say, He's more interested in why we live His life through us.

This is the ever-unfolding journey of finding God's life for my will. Yes, you read that right. I didn't say His will for my life. He's made that perfectly clear:

- His will for my life is joy.
- His will for my life is rest.
- His will for my life is forgiveness, gratitude, and purity of heart.

No. I'm after something different.

His life for my will, and yours, is a never-ending process of submission. His life for my will and yours is the slow, arduous, and oftentimes painful journey of surrender, where He inspects our motivations and not just our behavior. Where He truly understands our mistakes and our successes.

Ask yourself, *Am I letting God use me, or am I trying to use Him? Am I trying to change God or letting Him change me?*

I want His life to change my will.

And hopefully yours too.

Jordan River or Red Sea?

Everyone thinks of changing the world,
but no one thinks of changing himself.

—LEO TOLSTOY

It took me way too long to figure out that I should marry my wife, Kelly. To some, we were still married quite young. I was twenty-seven and she was twenty-six when we finally said "I do." We dated for three and a half years, though. And looking back, I think we dated precisely three years and three months too long. She was beautiful and funny; she loved God, her friends, puppies, mountains, and the elderly. She was perfect. Yet I just couldn't bring myself to pop the question. On paper, she was flawless, but what if she was tricking me? I was a theater major in college, so I knew a thing or two about pretending. What if we got a few days into the honeymoon and she removed the mask? What if underneath all that kindness and warmth, she was actually a tyrannical mutant? I mean, love knows no boundaries, but there were some things I couldn't live with. Wasn't marriage about finding a perfect person for you? I needed to be absolutely certain. I didn't want an ounce of guesswork when it came to who I would be with for the rest of my life.

At the two-and-a-half-year mark, I sat on my bed and struggled with the song I was writing. It wasn't really a song, I admit. It was more an argument than a composition. But that's always been the way I write songs. I bring my questions, and my guitar brings her six strings, and I let the two of them wrestle it out. That's exactly what I was doing one not-so-ordinary South Florida day.

I brooded on, as a typical afternoon thunderstorm raged outside my window. I was storming on the inside. I scribbled away in my journal, desperately trying to convince my heart to quit freaking out and hoping that God would give me the answer I was looking for. A simple yes or no would have sufficed, but try as I might, my heart was still in upheaval, and the Almighty wasn't talking. "Just tell me what to do!" I screamed between verses. "I don't need to know anything else—just give me this one answer!" It didn't help that I had recently graduated from a private Christian college. It seemed that my friends were all receiving words from the Lord left and right, while all I got was His cold shoulder. "Thanks, Jesus," I said, pouting. "I thought I was Your boy." Even though I knew I loved my girlfriend, I didn't think my love was enough of a reason to jump in. I needed a divine green light from the Maker Himself. Why couldn't He do that? He parted the Red Sea, after all. He certainly could part my worry and grant me a little bit of peace. What was He waiting for? My conundrum continued.

I knew I had to make a choice. A few months earlier, we had actually broken up for the fifth and what felt like the final time. Yes, my wife and I broke up five times while we were dating. I'm telling you, it's a miracle we made it. There was a myriad of reasons for our other breakups, but this time the reason was simple. I couldn't commit. The day before I was supposed to get on a plane and ask her father for her hand in marriage, I backed out. Ouch. In my weak defense, I didn't technically back out. I simply told my soon-to-be fiancée that I was scared to death. Shockingly, she didn't like that. I guess a woman doesn't like to hear that her man is unsure the day before he's asking for her hand in marriage. Imagine that. The next day she justifiably got on the plane to Michigan without me, and I, also justifiably, stayed home in my fog of indecision.

Somehow I talked her into dating me again but soon found myself right back where I had started. I was still scrounging for peace to make the move into matrimony. Why couldn't I get it together? I beat my head against the top of my guitar. Was this some sort of artist's unconscious self-sabotage? Was I in love with my doubt more than my faith? Was I making things harder than they needed to be for creativity's sake? Some old David Wilcox lyrics played in my head: "I was mourning the loss of the choices I'd lose."[1] Exactly. Choosing her meant not choosing anyone else. I was terrified. Saying yes to this girl meant saying no to every other girl down the road. What if my future soul mate was about to descend on a white horse from heaven, but I jumped the gun?

I threw my guitar down and put my running shoes on. Disgusted, I heaved myself out the front door and ran headlong into the storm. The thunder and lightning outside perfectly reflected the tempest raging inside me. I started running in spite of the pouring rain. I've found that sometimes when you're stuck in a spiritual standoff, the best thing to do is to stop waiting for permission and start moving.

So I did.

I didn't even care that I was getting soaked. I didn't think twice about the mixture of tears, rain, and snot streaming down my face. I just kept going. I was still living in West Palm Beach at the time—which, by the way, is one of the greatest places to go for a run—and before I knew it I had covered a couple of miles. Three miles passed, then four. Apparently, panic is a fantastic performance enhancer. I traversed back alleys and a few neighborhoods until I began my ascent of the intercoastal bridge. I was charging up and over the precipice like an angry, bellowing rhinoceros when the rain suddenly stopped. The clouds parted. Sunrays streamed through holes in the clouds and danced down across the water. I slowed my gait to a jog, then a walk. Soon I came to a dead stop at the top of the bridge. My friend Caleb used to say of this oceanic occurrence, "The fish are getting out their sparklers." And they seemed to be. Standing there, soaked from head to toe, I caught my breath and stared out at nature's party unfolding before me.

Then God spoke.

And He completely avoided my question.

I'll never leave you nor forsake you, He whispered to my heart.[2]

"What?" I stammered, sweaty and out of breath.

I'll never leave you nor forsake you, He repeated.

"Cool," I shot back to the heavens. "But that's not what I asked!"

I work all things together for good for those who love Me and have been called according to My purpose. He was insistent.[3]

"Thanks, God," I responded with a snort. "Now You're just messing with me, aren't You?"

It went on like this for some time. Me standing exhausted on a bridge, annoyingly arguing with the sky, and God flooding my mind with promise after promise. It's honestly a bit embarrassing to admit. I still don't know why it took me so long to see what God was doing, but slowly, steadily, surely, as He refused to give me the answer I was looking for, something I hadn't ever considered became quite clear. *Perhaps,* I thought, *God isn't giving me the plan because He wants to* be *the plan.*

Awkward silence.

Jumping into the Jordan

I married the girl in the end. Ten years in and four daughters later, I couldn't be happier about it. If you've met my wife, then you know I outkicked the coverage. And no, God never told me to marry her. At least, not in the way I thought He would. He never told me no, so I started walking toward yes. I stopped asking for an answer and moved based on what I knew was true. I guess you could say I stopped waiting for Him to part the Red Sea and decided to jump into the Jordan River. My friend Bob calls it "going

Grand Canyon." It's his way of approaching life as if he's sky-diving. Some big decisions look terrifying until you realize God's grace is strapped to your back like a parachute. I call it jumping into the Jordan because I had to let the currents of God's faithfulness wash away my fear that He wouldn't come through.

In case you're not familiar with the story, in the book of Exodus, we're told that God parted the Red Sea before the fleeing Israelites made it to the water's edge. Pharaoh's army thundered ominously behind, but God's chosen people walked across the sea's expanse on dry land. There wasn't even a drop on them.[4] In the book of Joshua, God also miraculously parted the Jordan River for the people, but that time it was different. In this story, God didn't make it quite so easy for His people. This time, some of them were going to have to get their feet wet. The priests carrying the ark of the covenant had to march straight into the unknown waters like Indiana Jones had to leap from the lion's head. Once they felt the cold reality of the river's current hit their sandaled feet, that's when God moved the waters.[5] Marrying Kelly was my jumping-into-the-Jordan moment. I never heard a no from God, so I just kept taking the next step. Before I knew it, the river had receded and I was dancing in the Promised Land. It was scary, uncomfortable, and euphoric. But it's what God had to demand of me to expose my fears.

Why does God do this? Why does He let me stand and watch some decisions part before me like the Red Sea but then other times force me to follow Him into the Jordan's unknowns? I don't have all the answers. But I do know that once I stopped asking God what I was supposed to do with my life and simply started asking how and why I was supposed to live my life, the seas of doubt began to part. In other words, I went with what I knew instead of letting what I didn't know paralyze me. This is essential. It's what marks our lives with faith. Instead of sitting stagnant at the water's edge, waiting for the miracle, we get up. We start working with what we do know.

The next time you're standing terrified on the shores of indecision, ask yourself what you know you should be doing. It could be as simple as giving thanks. It could be as demanding as selling off some possessions and giving the proceeds to the poor. It could be as impossible as forgiving someone before they even apologize. I don't know where you need to start, but I suggest starting with what you know. It's amazing the domino effect small acts of love can put into motion.

When it came to marrying my wife, I realized I needed to stop worrying if Kelly was the one and start worrying about how I would treat her if she were. I quickly surmised that dragging her along while I weighed all my other options was hardly the most loving thing I could do. Running across the bridge that day, I came to the hard realization that I would have to take the first steps of faithfulness toward her if I wanted to find out if she'd be faithful to me. Choosing her was not only something I had to do that day; it's something I've had to commit to doing every day since. I desperately wish more couples understood this. Love is action. It's a perpetual yes. After all, I know a lot of guys who begged God for an answer about who they should marry, and then it seems they stopped asking Him how they should love that girl every day since they received the answer they were looking for.

So what kind of moment are you in? If you're reading this book, there's a good chance you're currently swimming in some kind of indecision. Should you wait for the Red Sea to part or jump into the Jordan? Which is it gonna be? Sadly, I won't play God for you. I'm quite sure only the Holy Spirit can tell you what to do in the end. But consider this: God loves it when we move in faith. He loves when we don't have all the answers but we act as though we trust that He does. So whether you're waiting or wading forward, take heart. He has more plans for you than you have for yourself. And even better, He's the only one who tells the waters which way to run.

42 Trips to the Principal's Office

Times are bad. Children no longer
obey their parents, and everyone is
writing a book.

—MARCUS TULLIUS CICERO

A s a kid, I wasn't interested in answers. I was interested in
rebellion. I didn't take well to following rules, nutrition
labels, No Trespassing signs—they all seemed more like
suggestions to me. Put simply, I was a child rebel. I made my own
rules. I trespassed. I destroyed toys. I goofed around in class.
Once, at my uncle Danny's suggestion, I willingly ate an entire
bowl of dog food . . . and liked it. I guess you could say I had a gift
for distorting reality to fit my personal desires. My poor mother
amassed quite a few chronicles documenting my unruly antics,

including but not limited to getting lost at the Lincoln Memorial at the age of three, jumping off ten-foot diving boards before I knew how to swim, and—perhaps the most illustrious of all— what has come to be known as "The Disney World Incident." At the age of four, I was restrained by a plastic leash as my family enjoyed a leisurely exploration of the park. Obviously, I had an aversion to such parameters, so, as my mother recalls, I broke free. She remembers being surprised to see a child matching my exact description walking freely past her in the opposite direction. A few moments passed before she realized I had taken the leash off and successfully latched it onto some other random unsuspecting child. Were it not for the understanding parents of the afore- mentioned abductee and the gracious handling of the entire affair by the governing Disney World authorities, my mom might have been removed from the park and thrown in jail on kidnapping charges.

Much of my adolescence passed in this way. I grew up in the great Commonwealth of Virginia, in the small downtown of Fredericksburg, which is widely regarded as the site of the most overwhelming victory for the Southern armies in the Civil War. Fittingly, my friends and I made war on that town every day of our prepubescent lives. I would say we felt we had successfully conquered and ruled over every square inch of our city by the tender age of nine—all on single-gear bicycles, I might add.

I lived a few blocks away from my two best friends, Nate and Will. We cruised our Huffy bicycles up and down the city streets all day, every day. I'm not kidding—all day, every day. We would hang out with the homeless at the train station while watching the trains flatten nickels on the tracks. We'd cruise the canal path to Carl's, the legendary local ice-cream purveyor, and buy jumbo ice-cream cones. We'd loiter ominously outside William Street Market, singing bits from *West Side Story* while sipping Dr Pepper from glass bottles until dinnertime. Whatever trouble you could think up, we'd already thunk it and were already getting into it. We fell off roofs. We tumbled down hills. We got stitches . . . *so many* stitches.

I'll never forget helping Nate build the most absurdly steep bike ramp at the bottom of his absurdly steep street. Mind you, this was only a few weeks after I crashed my own bike into my four-year-old sister and knocked her two front teeth out. She didn't have front teeth for five years. Five years! You would have thought the incident would have slowed me down. Nope. Fourteen days later we were going bigger and better. As if it wasn't enough that the intersection at the bottom of Nate's street didn't have stop signs to halt cross traffic as we flew through, we decided to tempt fate further by sliding several plywood boards precariously atop a couple of two-foot-high logs. When Nate hit our makeshift Evel Knievel stunt track, going what my nine-year-old mind perceived as Mach 3, I remember thinking, *Wow. I've never seen someone airborne that long.* When he hit the pavement and his front wheel immediately bent in half like a taco, I remember exclaiming, "I've never seen someone skid across pavement that long." Nate's crash slowed him down for a week or two, but it didn't even put a dent in our love for tomfoolery. We remained ready for mischief. If there was trouble, we were undoubtedly in the midst of it.

In middle school, I continued on the same trajectory. During my seventh-grade year, I was sent to the principal's office forty-two times, which I presume must be the school record. Yes, *forty-two times*. I talked out of turn. I lit things on fire. I hopped up on my desk "O Captain! My Captain!" style[1] any time a teacher stepped out of the room. Were it not for the indelible wisdom of Randy Brunk, the presiding principal of my private Christian school, I might still be there, serving a life sentence in detention. Each time I was thrown out of class and into the chair outside his door, he would make me sit there for about twenty minutes before bringing me in. When he would finally call for me, he always started the same way: "Well, Michael, what brings you into my office today?"

Mr. Brunk was the first adult in my life, other than my parents, who spoke to me as an equal. He never talked down to me. When he spoke to me, he not only let me reply but also listened. I walked out of his office with plenty of demerits, but I also walked out each time feeling a little taller. Mind you, I'm well aware my behavior did not merit such courtesy, and I think that's precisely why it's worth mentioning. To this day, I still point to my talks with Randy as a marker of a rudimentary but profound shift in my life. It was the first time I can recall that an academic superior didn't seem hung up on my behavior issues but really wanted to focus on why I felt the need to act so stupidly. After all, it's easier to firmly hand down punishment on rule breaking than it is to gently guide a wild thirteen-year-old to psychoanalyze himself. Not many have the patience for that sort of thing. But Randy did.

The most striking example would have to be the time he caught me stealing from the school vending machine. I was down on the floor of the snack room in the gym, arm monkeyed up the candy-dispensing zone, desperately swinging my fingers at a package of Starbursts nestled perfectly within reach on the bottom row. That's exactly how Mr. Brunk found me as he turned the corner. Now, what did he have to say about my act of petty larceny? "Hmm . . . Michael. You're trying to tell me that your integrity is only worth fifty cents? Interesting. I always thought it was worth more than that." And with those few words, he turned around and left me alone. No detention. No community service. No time behind bars.

Granted, consequences have their place, but wisdom knows when to apply them and where those places are. He left me alone to silently examine my own heart. Years later, I realized he had perfectly embodied the quote, "Treat a man as he is, and he will remain as he is. Treat a man as he could be, and he will become what he should be." There's argument as to whether it was Goethe or Ralph Waldo Emerson who originally said that, but I can tell you, Randy was the first person in my life who applied it. He was the first teacher to use grace as discipline. Even though it would be another three years before I would read *Les Misérables* during my sophomore year of high school, Randy handed me my first real life "bishop and the candlesticks" kind of a moment. I was Jean Valjean, caught red-handed. Randy was the priest who threw in the silverware too. And it worked. I haven't stolen a single thing since.

I regularly thank God for Randy and for every other person

like him who has shown me a different way. Come to think of it, *Les Misérables* has even become my favorite book. I guess I relate to people who need a little mercy. And I equate people like Randy to those who are ready to wield grace as a teaching tool because they know only grace can truly melt a heart of stone.

Like Randy, my parents have always showered me with more unmerited favor than I could understand. Without their belief, compassion, and humor, I don't know where I'd be. Seriously, the fact that my mother never pulled out all her hair or had a mental breakdown is a tribute to the grace of God—as is the writing of this book. If you had told my mom thirty years ago this same son of hers—the one who was constantly falling from trees and running away from her any chance he could, the one who was sent to the principal's office forty-two times—would go on to advocate the beauty of surrendering his will, she might have just laughed in your face.

The following year, I changed. I don't exactly know what happened that summer, but over the course of my eighth-grade year, I wasn't sent to the principal even once. That's forty-two to zero for those of you keeping track. How could that be? Did my teachers throw in the towel and decide to let me go ahead and overthrow the teaching staff? Did puberty finally kick in and change my neurological wiring? Perhaps. But I think the real change was in my head. I started to believe what Mr. Brunk had been telling me every one of those times I visited his office the year before: "Your mistakes do not define you, Michael." Now, I don't know if he used those exact words or not, but I know those are the words that to this day are still burned into my soul. Though everyone else gave me the label of "troublemaker" in seventh grade, he gave me a different label to believe in. It was something like "child of God."

It would be another fifteen years before I would scribble down the chorus to a song called "You Are More" in my journal, but it was during the forty-two trips to the principal's office at age thirteen when those words began to take shape in my heart.

You are more than the choices that you've made
You are more than the sum of your past mistakes
You are more than the problems you create
You've been remade.[2]

The apostle Paul said it this way in 2 Corinthians 5:17: "If anyone is in Christ, he is a new creation. The old has passed away; behold, the new has come." I don't know what mistakes you see when you look in the mirror. But whoever you believe is looking back at you, rest assured that is who you will act like. Labels are powerful things. Maybe you never learned to look past the labels you were given at thirteen. Maybe you agreed with the mistakes you made, and that's who you've been ever since. Maybe you dreamed of having a principal like mine, because yours only told you who you would never be. Maybe you're hoping this time you'll finally get your act together. Maybe this will be the time you pick yourself up by your bootstraps and make yourself new. Maybe. Well, before you try to do that, I want to remind you what I learned as a middle school delinquent. Behavior follows the label, not the other way around. And the best part? You are a new creation right now, right where you stand, if you would simply believe it. You don't deserve it. In fact, none of us can deserve it. We only receive it. And when we receive the new name grace gives us, we begin to act like who we were made to be.

Now I have four daughters . . . pray for me. Having four girls in the house is great. It just means someone's crying and it's usually me. And no, I'm not praying for a boy. I've found the Lord gives girls to a family that already has a man. Hey O! But now that I'm a father, I'm intensely aware of how early we begin to believe our labels. Just a few days ago, after several willful displays of abject disobedience, my four-year-old groaned, "I always do everything wrong."

Hearing those words come out of her little mouth sent knives right through me. I knelt down and held her face gently in my hands. "No, baby," I countered firmly yet tenderly. "You made some bad choices today, but that is not who you are. You are a child of light, and tomorrow we get a new chance to act like it. Mercy is new every morning."

"Every morning?" she said, raising her sorrowful eyes to mine, endless pools of blue and possibility.

"Every morning, sweet girl. I know because I need it every morning too."

We hugged and I cried way more than she did. If I have any job on this earth, it is first and foremost to tell my sweet daughters every day who they get to be. After forty-two trips to Randy's office, I believe we all end up becoming who we believe we are. Or maybe I should say, *whose* we believe we are.

When Dreams Die

Sooner or later God'll cut you down.

—Johnny Cash, "God's Gonna Cut You Down"

Just two weeks before my eighteenth birthday, I was thrown from a car going fifty miles an hour. Wait. I should clarify. I wasn't thrown out, like by the mob or something. I was ejected. The car flipped. My body was thrown from the vehicle, and I hurled through the air in perfect accordance with the laws of physics.

The accident happened as most accidents do—unexpectedly. With only a few expletives from my friend's mouth and the accompanying symphony of screeching tires, the three of us—Jonny Rios, Sam Diehl, and I—found ourselves airborne. We were supposed to be on our way to school that morning, but as you might have guessed, we never made it.

The morning air was crisp and clean with the first few hints of fall. Our minds were alive with senioritis, whirring with the excitement and expectancy of our final year of high school. I guess you could say it was an otherwise perfect mid-September morning. At least it was until the front wheel of the two-door Honda CRX we had borrowed from our classmate Kevin caught the edge of the pavement on Mine Road. We skidded violently sideways, and any other plans we had made for our senior year were changed indefinitely.

I didn't have my seat belt on.

Witnesses said the car somersaulted through the air some five or six times before finally coming to rest in an elderly woman's lawn. I will have to trust their report on this, because I don't remember much of it. My best friend, Jonny, who was driving the car, tells me he heaved himself out of the driver's side window once the car finally came to rest. He spun around a few times trying to locate me. Just then, Sam, who had been sitting hunched up illegally in the car's hatchback when we ran off the road, ran up to Jonny without a scratch on him. Apparently, the trunk swung open while the car fishtailed off the road, and he was flung out as well, rolling only once on the ground before finding himself standing upright in the middle of the road. He pointed Jonny to my bloody body lying motionless on the pavement a few hundred feet away.

Jonny ran to me and was relieved to hear me moaning as he approached. Then he saw my face and was not so relieved. My face had been torn apart and blood poured from the gashes. The asphalt was quickly reddening around me.

People try to tell you what near-death experiences are like, and of course, the accounts always fall short. *Out-of-body* is an apt description, I would say. That's how I felt. Now, I'd like to tell you I saw my grandpa chilling at the pearly gates with Saint Peter, but no such luck. My experience was more like watching myself on an episode of *ER*. I remember the car slamming into a mailbox and the entire windshield violently shattering in a moment. It all happened so fast, I didn't even have time to panic. All I saw when I closed my eyes was the mailbox, and I heard the sound of glass breaking. After that, it all went dark.

The next thing I saw was the back of an ambulance. Had it been minutes? Hours?

My eyes squinted open to see paramedics' faces hovering over me. They started hammering me with questions. "What's your name?"

"Mike?" My answer was more of a question than a statement. I honestly wasn't quite sure.

"What month is it?"

My face contorted.

"Who is the president?"

I didn't know.

Blackout.

I opened my eyes to the perfect rhythm of florescent bulbs passing overhead in a hospital corridor. I thought I might have remembered moving from the ambulance, because an image of the sky filled with birds kept flickering in and out of my mind as I counted lights above. "One, two, three . . ." My stomach lurched as I felt the stretcher fly down the hall.

Blackout.

My vision came back slowly. This time as a gentle fade from black to my parents' haggard faces. They were huddled up next to me, and they were crying. To this day, this is the first time I remember feeling afraid. These are the moments you're used to your parents being brave for you. My parents' courage had run out. They handed me something in a cup. They were telling me to drink it. "It will help the doctors see your insides," they said. I gulped it down. The room spun. Before I knew it, I was back under.

Blackout.

I woke to the soft pulsing tone of a heart monitor in my hospital room.

Beep. Beep. Beep.

The cadence was calming. My eyes focused in the dark room. I saw a digital clock reading 12:43. *Is that a.m. or p.m.? Is that a clock, or is it some sort of medical device? Where am I?* A nurse walked in, and I was suddenly aware of the crippling pain coursing through my body. I croaked out to him, "Excuse me. Can you turn me on my side? My back hurts so bad . . . I can't take it." He nodded and approached the bed. Instead of turning me, he reached up to the plastic bag hanging next to my bed. I felt the cold fire sweep through my arm where I could now see the IV attached. The morphine snaked its way across my chest and through my back.

Blackout.

A few days later, I finally came to for more than a few moments. Other family members and friends had begun visiting. The first full conversation I can recall is the one with my doctor. He nonchalantly explained to me how I had been flung from the car when it flipped. He said I hit my chest on the ground so hard the impact had fractured two of my vertebrae. My skull was also fractured on my right side where my ear had been ripped off. I remember frantically reaching for my ear as he smiled for the first time. He told me a plastic surgeon had been able to reattach it seamlessly. "Your two friends who were in the car with you are both fine," he reassured me. "Looks like you got the worst of it, but it sure was lucky how you were thrown out." He then proceeded to show me a picture of the car we were in. "The roof of the car was crushed all the way down to your seat. If you had stayed in, you'd have been a goner."

My face scrunched as I stared at the Polaroid. "I should be . . . dead?"

"Well, I wouldn't say you should be dead," the doctor said. "You obviously should be alive. The EMTs said you did die, actually. Flatlined five times on your way here is what they told me." He pointed to the ceiling and chuckled. "Seems to me Someone up there must want you around for you to have survived that! But," he mumbled, switching gears, "looks like you'll be lying around for quite a while. I'd say at least two months on your back. You may be able to walk by then, but I wouldn't count on it. And, oh, I'd rule out any dream of athletics if I were you . . . most likely, indefinitely."

Bone Growth

My life up to that point was a constant flurry of activity. I ran from sport to sport, event to event, and rarely, if ever, stopped. I would often forget to eat because I was too busy living. If "fear of missing out" had been a meme back then, I could have been the poster child.

Being told I would probably never run again was like being handed a death sentence. The room caved in. Sweat flooded my face. "I . . . may . . . never . . . run . . . again?" I spoke each word as slowly as I could, rolling them around in my mind, perhaps in an effort to rewind the tape and have the doctor change his prognosis.

"Yeah, but yesterday we thought you wouldn't last the night. Just this morning there were talks you'd never walk again. I'd be happy to be alive if I were you. Crazy you're still here at all."

To be perfectly honest, I know I should have been astonishingly grateful to be alive at that moment, but I wasn't. I wasn't happy at all. I was angry. I mean, why would I be saved from something like that only to be told my life would never be as good as it once was? What seventeen-year-old has time to appreciate what they have when everything else has been taken away?

The questions bombarded me from every angle. *Why weren't my friends hurt? Why was I the only one lying there with my face torn off? If God could save me from death, why couldn't He save me from injury? Was He up in heaven explaining, "Well, there's a difference between mostly dead and all dead"?*

I absolutely couldn't see even a sliver of hope at the time.

After my weeklong stint in the ICU, I was released to go home. There, I was confined to my bed and sentenced to death by stillness. Or so it seemed. Apparently, the only way for my compression fractures to heal was to lie motionless on my back and stare at my bedroom ceiling.

You need to understand, even though I'm quite sure I'm a Enneagram type four, I come across to many as a classic type seven—high spirited, enthusiastic, spontaneous, and energetic. To me, being stationary and confined to bed felt like nothing short of purgatory. In all, I lay there for six long weeks, waiting and waiting for my bones to heal. But during those six weeks, not only was I smothered under a cloud of depression, but I was also blanketed by boredom. I was crazy bored—as in talking-to-my-little-brother's-stuffed-animals bored.

What happened next was the planting of a future miracle. Yes, it was already a miracle I was alive, but I wouldn't recognize this other miracle as such until years later. I asked for a guitar. I know that sounds like a strange detour in the story, and it probably doesn't sound much like a miracle, but trust me when I say it would one day produce another shift in the course of my life. Asking for a guitar didn't feel like any sort of monumental decision. It was simply a way to pass the time and not go insane doing it. Little did I know, as one dream died, another was beginning to push its way through the dirt.

My parents obliged and bought me an acoustic Seagull guitar. I was overjoyed . . . and terrible, I might add. Ask any of my classmates from high school, and they'll tell you. I still remember the confused looks on my friends' faces at our ten-year reunion. "You're doing what now? But you were so . . . bad!"

When I first tried to play bar chords, it sounded like cats dying—slowly. And painfully. Later in the year, while practicing in a corner of the gym, I was actually asked to stop by the coach of the girls' basketball team. "The team can't concentrate with you making noises like that! It's wrong and ungodly. You should be ashamed of yourself. I award you no points, and may God have mercy on your soul."

Okay. He didn't say all that, but it was close. I was terrible at playing guitar, no question, but at least I wasn't bored! I'd rather be terrible and entertained than have my mind be unoccupied. The guitar had finally given me something to do. I had a purpose.

A beginner, three-hundred-dollar Canadian guitar saved me from despondency, and it would actually go on to shape the trajectory of the rest of my life. Never in a million years would I have thought a piece of wood and six strings could change the course of my future, but it did. For the next few months after my close brush with death, I sat on my bed day after day and slowly worked my way through chord sheets and song charts. My bones grew strong, but my heart grew stronger. Learning to play guitar shifted my heart from despair to dedication, and it slowly taught my soul how to rest in the process.

By Christmastime, I was back up on my feet and running around again. Shockingly, I proved my doctor wrong and played basketball on my high school team that year. But sports were no longer my first and only love. Music had come and met me when I needed healing most.

It would be almost fifteen years later that I would write the words, "I want to know a song can rise from the ashes of a broken life . . ." But that is literally what happened to me. I know now that God is unbelievably, wondrously, annoyingly patient, and His grace, though strong, true, and unstoppable, can also work in slow, meandering, and even painfully mysterious ways. Breaking my back that fall day in September was the event that would eventually lead me to signing a record deal and one day singing all over the world. Crazy.

I just have to shake my head as I write this, because sometimes the greatest things in our lives are born from the worst. Sometimes the moments of greatest tragedy are the exact moments when something beautiful is being born. And sometimes the only thing keeping us from God's dreams for our lives is our unwillingness to let go of how we thought our own dreams should go.

Dreams Change
(and That's Okay)

God is always trying to give good things to
us, but our hands are too full to receive them.

—SAINT AUGUSTINE, *THE CITY OF GOD*

B ecause I have four daughters, I am well versed in all things "princess." It's only fitting. The boy who spent his childhood terrorizing the neighborhood is now being subjected to dress-up and afternoon tea. Justice comes for us all, I guess. So naturally, a few months ago, our family was watching *Tangled*, Disney's animated take on "Rapunzel," when a line jumped out at me. Forgive me if you haven't seen it, but let me go ahead and ruin it for you. There's a moment when Flynn Rider, the bad boy turned good and the romantic lead, sings out that his dream is to live on a secluded island surrounded by piles of money. Moments later, a burly, uneducated, scary-looking fella helps Flynn and Rapunzel escape. But before he leads them down to a secret trap-door, he says, "Go. Live your dream!" When Rider says "I will," Burly Man shuts him down. "Your dream stinks," he states flatly. "I was talking to her."[1]

Consider another cinematic proverb. In *Monsters University*, we see the developing friendship of Mike Wazowski, the "no mat-ter how hard you try or how much you know, you'll never be a scarer," and his classmate Sulley, the "never worked hard a day in your life, but you're naturally talented and it's not fair because that's what Mike wants with all his heart, and he's actually study-ing and doing everything he can to earn it, but you're naturally scarier so you get to be the hero" guy. I was shocked at the take-away from this "kids' movie." Again, I'm sorry I'm ruining an-other one for you, but in the end, Mike has to come to terms with the fact he's just flat out *not scary*. Providentially, he does end up realizing his dream of working on the scare floor but not at all in the capacity he envisioned. He didn't become a scarer, but instead he was an incredible assistant to one. His passion was there, but his role was different than he had dreamed. This is radical.

Many of us believe the opposite. We tend to propagate the common cultural ideology that we can do whatever we dream of doing and be anything we want to be. But that's simply not true. I mean, I can't transform myself into an eagle and fly off a roof (though I did try that when I was seven). I can't turn myself into a rocket scientist if I don't have the education and intellectual capac-ity to fill that role.

Most personality tests and skills assessments conclude the

same. Can you get better in areas where you're not naturally wired to excel? Sure. Should you do things you're terrible at? Absolutely. But are those the best places to focus all your vocational energy? Maybe not. Mark Twain once quipped, "The secret of success is making your vocation your vacation." You do better to hone in on the ways your mind tends to work and get even better in those areas. You'll also learn the humility required to rely on others who are gifted in ways you're not.

We can be much more than what many might give us credit for, but I don't think it's emotionally responsible to make a sweeping blanket statement like, "You can do anything you put your mind to!" But what I can do is say, "Okay, God, I have these dreams and these desires and talents, and they seem to be leading me in a particular direction. So show me where they need to shift and change to be Your dreams and Your desires." Sometimes I've found that they line up better than I could have imagined, but other times I've felt like God has had to say to me, "Mike, your dream stinks."

The Greatest of All Time

As a ten-year-old who loved all things sports, I dreamed of playing for the Boston Celtics. My dad grew up in Boston, so his deep reverence for Larry Bird transferred to me early on. Sitting on the floor by my father's feet, I watched those epic battles of the 1980s between the Celtics and the Lakers, and I was mesmerized. Even before I could talk, I would scream at the TV right along with him. Johnson and Bird. Magic and Larry. The rivalry was a thing of legend. It seemed that no matter how the game went, whoever had the ball last was going to win. Deep in my ten-year-old heart, I knew one day I too would hoist the championship trophy in Boston Garden, and Larry Bird would ask me to come hang at his house and play long games of H-O-R-S-E in his backyard under a beautiful sunset. I would often tear up at the sweet vision in my mind of my jersey hanging from the rafters next to his.

The summer before my fourth-grade year, our family suddenly moved across town away from my two best friends, Nate and Will. I was still in sackcloth and ashes over the whole ordeal when my dad decided to put up a hoop in the driveway of the new house. Overnight, my sorrow turned to rejoicing, my weeping into song. I was still bummed to be moving away from downtown, but I would be back one day. And I would return a basketball savant.

For the entire next year, I made a commitment to myself to make a hundred foul shots a day. Even if I had to shoot five hundred, I wouldn't let myself come inside until I had drained a century's worth. Every day after school? Foul shots. Early Saturday mornings before cartoons? Foul shots. Rain? Foul shouts. Snow? Foul shouts. Tsunami? Foul shouts. Whatever a given day could throw at me, I'd be out in the driveway, tossing that ball from the free-throw line.

Fantasy overtook me. The commentator in my head was my biggest fan. "Game 7, no time left on the clock. Donehey has just been fouled, unthinkably. I can't imagine the stress he's under, Bob. The team is down by one. If he makes both shots, they're the champs. He makes the first! And . . . oh! He misses the second . . . But wait! He tips in his own miss before the buzzer!"

All afternoon I'd daydream about sinking game-winning shots, being hoisted on my teammates' shoulders. And one day, perhaps, just perhaps, my name might even be mentioned in the much-coveted conversation about the Greatest Player of All Time.

Now, I might mention this took place before I reached my formidable five-foot-eight adult frame. Like Mike Wazowski, I too had to come to terms with my own limitations. I do still hoop it up from time to time, but it's not at the Garden. It's twice a week at my local YMCA. You can still find me out there next to the aerobics class, raining threes. I don't want to brag, but one magic day when my shot was falling, I was referred to in a pickup game as The Great White Hope. So I've got that going for me, which is nice.

It's crazy how time changes things, though. As an adult, I view the game so much differently than I did as an overly optimistic kid. Even the reasons I play the game are different. I used to play to prove my existence had worth. Now I play to keep my body from becoming decrepit. It's a new agenda, a new reality.

But the more I change, the more ESPN remains the same. If you were to turn on ESPN any time of the day or year, I bet you'd still hear the phrase "the greatest of all time" within fifteen minutes. Jordan, Kobe, Russell, Lebron, Chamberlain, Magic, Bird . . . the list goes on, and the analysts love the debate. More important than the number of championship rings, salary, or the fact that it's a good form of exercise, definitely more important than motivation and personal integrity, our obsession with basketball is figuring out who was the greatest ever to play the game. After all, what could possibly be more important than being the

G.O.A.T? We buy in, as I did at an early age. Most of us don't even consider an alternative.

I have a friend who plays in the NBA. Now, before you think I'm name-dropping to sound cool, I'll be sure not to tell you his name. Besides, the last time I saw him, he picked me up and swung me around like a rag doll. Trust me, I did not feel cool. I felt like a hobbit. So my unnamed professional basketball-playing friend knows Michael Jordan. They've hung out. I don't think they're besties or anything, but they've been around each other on a consistent basis. Many people consider Michael Jordan to be the greatest ever. Whether you agree or not, it would be mandatory to at least mention his name in the conversation. Well, my friend told me Michael is one of the unhappiest basketball players he's ever met. I said, "What on earth are you talking about? *The* Michael Jordan? *Six championships* Michael Jordan? *Gatorade song* Michael Jordan? *The guy whose silhouette is on your stinking shoes* Michael Jordan? *Space Jam* MICHAEL JORDAN? *I Believe I Can Fly* MICHAEL JORDAN! How could he not be happy?" My friend insists, "I'm telling you. His worth was so wrapped up in playing basketball, and now that he can't play anymore, he's deeply unhappy."

You can believe my friend or not, but the questions still loom. Don't just ask yourself what would happen if your basketball dreams were dashed like mine. Take it a step further. What if you got everything you dreamed of? What if you attained every dream and goal you ever had? Would you finally be happy? Would I? Is it more important to be the greatest at something or to love what you do? What if you have to change what you love to do?

Since I'm a father myself now, I have to articulate these things to my daughters. After having kids, I realized only adults don't dance. Did you know that? I've never met a kid who was physically able, who didn't dance. But adults who don't dance? They're a dime a dozen. Why? Because somewhere along the line someone told them they weren't good at it. We think the only things worth doing are the things that we're good at. Hogwash. The sooner you give up being the greatest, the sooner you can experience the freedom of flailing around a room with your daughter giggling at the top of her lungs.

But many of us stop dancing because we're not really great at it. If that's the case, then it begs the question: Why are you doing only the things you're good at? Is it enough to do what we really love doing, or do we do it only if it's something other people deem a big deal? If you ever get the chance, I highly recommend you read Andre Agassi's autobiography, *Open*. In it, he chronicles the incessant pressure that pulverized him throughout his career because he didn't truly love the game of tennis. Rather, he felt as though he had to keep up the image. This coming from a man who accomplished about as much in the tennis world as any one person could.

So how much is enough to finally feel like you've made it? In *Mere Christianity,* C. S. Lewis points out, "Pride gets no pleasure out of having something, only out of having more of it than the next man."[2] I have to deal with this. If it's true, then wanting to be the greatest of all time and highly esteemed by the anchors on SportsCenter is actually a terrible motivation. It's a stinky dream. Or maybe I should say it's a weak dream. In essence, I'm saying, "I can't be happy being my personal best to the glory of God. I can only be happy if my personal best is better than everybody else's."

Speaking of the greatest, I'll never forget watching Tom Brady (I told you my dad's from Boston, right?) in a *60 Minutes* interview look quizzically back at the camera after being asked what it felt like. This was even before his record-setting sixth Super Bowl win. Steve Kroft was interviewing him, and they talked about his Super Bowl rings, all the superstars he was compared to, his career. Then Steve asked, "This whole experience—this whole upward trajectory—what have you learned about yourself? What kind of an effect does it have on you?"

Looking up to who knows where, Tom responded in puzzlement, "Why do I have three Super Bowl rings, and still think there's something greater out there for me? I mean, maybe a lot of people would say, 'Hey man, this is what is.' I reached my goal, my dream, my life. Me, I think: God, it's gotta be more than this. I mean this can't be what it's all cracked up to be. I mean I've done it. I'm 27. And what else is there for me?"[3]

WHAT? What else is there? Are you kidding me, Tom? Winning Super Bowls, dating supermodels, isn't that living the dream? Apparently not. Being the greatest isn't enough for Tom Brady. It's not enough for Michael Jordan. And if being the greatest isn't enough for them, then what dream do we think will be enough for us?

I went to college the year after my car accident. My fractured vertebrae had healed, but any dream of a future in professional sports was shattered beyond repair. And not even on account of my accident, but really just on the merit of my general lack of skill.

So I turned to acting. I had always been in the school play every spring growing up, and I had even attended a theater arts program called Governor's School the summer before my car crash. I felt like being famous would be cool, so I decided upon my new and certain career path. And I enrolled in college as an overconfident, attention-hungry theater major. In retrospect, it's amazing how similar my story was to Mike Wazowski's. I was going to be onstage, just not the way I thought.

My high school theater teacher was and still is a vivacious and high-spirited woman named Chris Barham. She had God-sized dreams for everyone she encountered. She still does, and I love that about her. I never said it was wrong to have a dream come true. It's only when we must have our dreams realized that we set ourselves up for disillusionment.

Chris never stopped dreaming. She had an insatiable thirst and appreciation for theater. Since she was an alum of James Madison University, I figured it would be a great college option for me too. I auditioned there and was accepted. The future was bright.

But Chris unknowingly threw a wrench into my collegiate plans when she asked me to portray a German pastor in our school play at the very end of my senior year of high school. She came to me earlier that winter and said, "Mike, I need to ask you something. I have a play I want to do. It's called *The Beams Are Creaking*. It's a play about Dietrich Bonhoeffer, and I wanted to ask you if you think you're up for playing the lead character. This is your last year, your last role before college, but I need to warn you. Playing Bonhoeffer will mess you up."

She had no idea how true that would be.

I eagerly agreed and assured her I was up for the challenge. How hard could it be? Getting ready for the role, though, I had to read almost everything the German pastor ever wrote. I had no idea what I was getting myself into. Now if you've ever studied him, you might guess how revolutionary this was. Memorizing Bonhoeffer's musings did something to my soul. If you don't know anything about this guy, you need to understand how resolved he was. He stood up to the Nazi Party and the state church until his death. The brilliance of his life shed light on the infidelity of the national German Evangelical Church, and it also exposed my own superficial plans and acting ambition. Granted, I still wasn't sure what I was going to do with my life, but reading robust remarks like his got under my skin in a hurry. One line in particular still makes the hairs on my arms stand up: "We are not to simply bandage the wounds of victims beneath the wheels of injustice, we are to drive a spoke into the wheel itself."[4] Mind you, this is coming from a pastor who was in on a plot to assassinate Hitler, so you know he meant it. I couldn't tell you I agreed with every stance he took, but as my director had warned, he most certainly messed me up.

I'm not exactly sure why, but I couldn't escape the thought that I needed to act for the glory of God, whatever that meant. I took some personal inventory of my dreams to act, and in a rather jarring last-minute decision, I switched colleges and went to Palm Beach Atlantic instead. PBA was a small, private, faith-based college with what I perceived as a theater program desperately in need of my acting prowess. It's grown substantially since my time there, so I'm chuckling as I reminisce. I was quite cocky. Certainly, this obscure Florida beach college was going to be eternally grateful for the forthcoming blessing my sweet acting skills would provide.

You know what happened? I didn't get a part in any of the school plays. I didn't get one single part my freshman year, and I auditioned for everything imaginable. Twice they told me they really wanted to cast me, but another kid looked the part. I was essentially told, "Sorry, kid, maybe next time." My sophomore year was much the same. I auditioned for every production possible, and I think I had a total of three or four speaking lines. Needless to say, I was destroyed. I was angry and confused. I know, I know. First-world problems. But deep down I think I always knew I wasn't going to be a professional athlete. I was pretty good at sports, but I was never the best. But in my small acting world in high school, I thought I was the next Brad Pitt. Letting go of this dream was something else entirely. If I was the best at something, how dare anyone thwart my greatness? Regardless of my less-than-pious motivations, I genuinely believed I would be a famous actor one day. Why wouldn't God just open up the path for me to do what I loved and something I was so obviously awesome at doing?

Even after studying Bonhoeffer messed up which college I would attend, I began my freshman year still clinging to a very particular plan for my life. I knew I was God's gift to acting, and nothing was going to keep me from realizing my dreams. But the unthinkable happened. No one recognized my genius! The concrete plan I had conjured up was erroneously deterred. (I know now I needed humbling.) But here's the annoying and the beautiful thing. I didn't get any meaningful roles in any of those plays, right? Well, because I wasn't in those rehearsals, I had a lot more free time to practice and write songs. I even had time to begin playing shows with the little band some buddies and I started in our dorm room. During my junior and senior years, I found myself turning down acting roles because this band we had begun in our spare time was being asked to play music all over the state of Florida. Remember that little guitar I had asked for when I was confined to my bed? Well, that guitar and that little band became my current profession.

Follow Desire Deeper Down

To me, it often seems like the plan we think God has for us is the very one He's asking us to let Him undo. It's excruciating and often disorientating, but it's the way our hearts are made. If we would relax our grip, if we could just hold our big dreams with open hands, then God could give and take away as He pleases, and our hearts could grow in the way they were meant to: in the steady evergreen soil of trust in God. But when we clench our fists and white-knuckle our dreams to the size and shape we've decided on, we end up squeezing the life right out of them. Francis Chan teaches, "[In following Jesus] you start learning that all the things that He's saying let go of and walk away from—those are actually things that were gonna destroy you anyway."[5]

This is undoubtedly true of me. I was so overly confident in my acting, I cringe to think of what might have happened to me if I did get famous. It's the same reason I find myself praying for the child actors on the cast of *Stranger Things*. If I had become famous that young, I would have ended up becoming the Demogorgon. Well, maybe I wouldn't have become an actual human-devouring slug monster, but my soul might have become something quite like it. Fame has a way of doing that. It exposes the brokenness inside us and then gives our pride something equivalent to Miracle-Gro.

Music, paradoxically, had the exact opposite effect on my ego. I was so aware of my deficiency in actual skill that every time I was asked to perform onstage, I felt like there was no explanation other than the grace of God. I don't know if I could say the same thing if I had gotten those leading roles early on.

Don't misunderstand me. The times God has asked me to let go of my dreams never felt like love when they were happening. In fact, a broken back or thwarted acting career can feel like nothing more than unnecessary obstacles getting in the way of true happiness. But the longer I live and the more I've had to let go of, the more I find God is always giving me more when He asks me to hold less. What He offers isn't more money or more fame necessarily, but it is absolutely more of what I need most. I'm not talking about bigger platforms and greater influence; I'm talking about things like joy, peace, and the rest that come from His presence.

Burrito Dreams

It's like Chipotle. I never wanted to try Chipotle. I remember when the first one was built in our town and my sisters would always try to get me to go there. When I was sixteen, I even worked at a Hollywood Video directly next door to one. (Kids, let me explain. Hollywood Video was like a Redbox the size of a whole store.) Not once in the entire year I worked there did I ever walk through the door one building over and give Chipotle a go. It wasn't because I didn't like the taste of the food. I didn't know what it tasted like. I would not try it—and this is embarrassing to admit—because I didn't like how the word sounded. Yup. I was a pronunciation snob. For whatever reason, it bothered me how no one could agree on how to pronounce the word *Chipotle*. Some people put the *l* before the *t*. They said, "Chi-Pole-Tey!" Other people called it "Chi-pot-el." I know it's so stupid, but I was convinced there was no delight waiting for me within that restaurant's walls. If they couldn't agree on what it was called, surely they wouldn't have the mind power to come up with exquisite-tasting cuisine. Then one day while home from college on Christmas break, my whole family went there after church, and I was forced to try it. A river of joy came rushing into my life.

What wonders! What glories had eluded me! My taste buds danced and swooned! My heart was enraptured. I was Bob Wiley in *What About Bob?* I cried out in ecstasy. I wept in euphoric bursts of simultaneous wonder and regret that I hadn't tasted the godly nectar of ethically raised meats and fresh vegetables sooner! It's still hard to accept all the times I missed out on so much culinary revelation because I arrogantly thought I knew my own taste buds. Chipotle, forgive me! I shut you out before I truly knew you!

From that day until now, I swore to myself my lunch choices would change forever. Just the other day, I drove severely out of the way to experience this fast-food marvel. Isn't that interesting? My lunch dreams and desires, silly as it sounds, didn't know what they were hungry for until they experienced what was beautiful and good.

So it is with our lives before God. The psalmist tells us in Psalm 37:4, "Delight yourself in the LORD, and he will give you the desires of your heart." It's shocking how quickly some will distort this as a call to strong-arm God. This is not a promise from God to give you whatever you want. It is, however, a promise that what we want will become God Himself.

Notice as you delight in God, just as you delight in anything, that delight will shift what your heart wants more of. Before God gives us what we want, He changes what we want, until He is all we want. He changes our taste buds, spiritually speaking. So before we demand that He give us the desires of our hearts, we do well to first demand that our hearts are in line with what He wants. We must hand over our dreams and desires first. We then anticipate, as we show Him our dreams, that He'll be faithful to change our dreams. Perhaps we'll find we didn't even know what it was we were asking for in the first place.

It's important here to mention that not only does He change some of our desires, but He also gives us the peace to live with unrealized desires. Our patience grows. When we taste and see God, we get better at waiting. Getting a taste of Him gives us new taste buds and makes us snobs in some ways, I suppose. It's like a pour-over coffee versus a Keurig. Once you've tasted the sweet glory of a carefully crafted cup of caffeine, you don't care how much longer it takes. You will wait for the best over settling for a quick fix.

Frustratingly, the ways of God are often all about delayed

gratification. Tasting God changes our wayward desires and allows us to go longer with unrealized good desires, as well. If I'm about to have an incredible cup of coffee, I will joyfully wait for it. It's a crude example, for sure, but it's true. For a couple waiting for their adoption to come through or a cancer fighter waiting on a clean bill of health, having the expectation of fulfillment makes the waiting far more manageable.

Good things are easier to wait for when we know the best is always coming. Isn't that what we say we believe? No matter how long God keeps us waiting, we still get Him in the end. Isn't that worth it?

This side of eternity, we must follow our desires deeper down. For instance, when we say "I want to be famous!," we think we know exactly what we're asking for. But God starts digging. When He looks in our hearts, He might see that our desire to be famous is really a misplaced dream of wanting to be known and loved. I know that's definitely true of me. So He may not put us on the cover of *People* magazine, but He will be faithful to put people in our lives we can trust and love and be known by. We pray, "Make me an incredible success story!" What we don't realize is we're actually hungry for acceptance. So we go about working ourselves to the bone and wonder why we don't feel a part of something meaningful. Meanwhile, God is offering us true community, but it will come only at the expense of saying no to certain career opportunities. He has an incredible way of giving us exactly what we always wanted, but it comes at the expense of taking away what we currently think we want.

I'm always fascinated by what my prayers reveal about what I think I need to be happy. Others' prayers teach me the same thing. So when I stumbled across the prayer of a king in the book of Proverbs, I took note. A king, after all, has everything this world would have us believe would make us happy. Money, fame, power . . . a king takes his pick. So King Agur's prayer in Proverbs 30 is especially jolting to me: "Give me neither poverty nor riches; feed me with the food that is needful for me, lest I be full and deny you and say, 'Who is the LORD?' or lest I be poor and steal and profane the name of my God" (verses 8–9).

WHAT. ON. EARTH?

Yeah. He prayed that. *No, really?* Yes, he did: "God, don't let me get poor, and don't let me get rich. If I get poor, I might curse You; if I get rich, I might forget You." I don't think I need to reiterate how mind-blowingly different this is from most people's daily requests before the Lord. Have you ever asked yourself this question: Would I take riches if it meant forgetting God? Some of you might not even blink. *Yep. Absolutely. I may forget Him, but He won't forget me, and He's loving and forgiving and all that, so I'll get the world and I'll get God in the end, anyway!* Not so fast.

In his exceedingly intuitive work *David and Goliath,* Malcolm Gladwell uncovers the astonishing U-shaped graph as it relates to wealth and happiness. Basically, a bunch of people were polled, and it turns out, if you have no money, you won't be happy. But just when you would assume that the converse is true, the statistics astound. Money seems to buy happiness but only to a point. The level of happiness goes up and up with every income level reported until you reach somewhere between $70,000 and $100,000 a year. Then you know what happens? The graph takes a plummet like a roller coaster. The more you make after that tax bracket? Statistically, happiness comes crashing down.[6]

If you ask me, this proves that Francis Chan, King Agur, and Gladwell are all onto the same thing. There is a sweet contentment that comes from living in a perpetual state of need and fulfillment from God's provision. If you're constantly worried about where your next meal is coming from, it's hard to rest. It's also intensely difficult to rest when you've lost touch with your need for God. As Agur stated, we're in a tightrope tension between forgetting God and cursing Him.

We seldom realize that it might be God's providence when we don't achieve certain successes that would be terrible for our souls. When were you last grateful for not reaching a certain income level? Perhaps our ache to have a certain amount of money in our bank accounts—or to be heralded as a great business success, teacher, real estate agent, or whatever—might actually be our souls' deeper hunger to be a part of something bigger than ourselves. Isn't that why we snap up copies of *People* magazine or read the latest celebrity gossip? We're made for the glory of God, and if we don't feel a certain participation in it, keeping tabs on famous people is the next best thing. It doesn't last, though. A person can't give us a glory big enough to satisfy our souls. A fat bank account can't do it either. Last I checked, nothing I can get this side of heaven will fill up this God-shaped hole inside me, so maybe I should relax a little bit and settle into the discontentment. Whatever it is I'm not yet receiving, I needn't be afraid when things don't turn out the way I planned. Chances are, as some dreams die, that's the exact moment when others are beginning to come alive.

Capitalistic Christianity

You're not the flower, but the vase
which holds the flower.
—JULIETTE BINOCHE

When I arrived at Palm Beach Atlantic University in the fall of 1999, guitar in tow and dreams intact, my life was an open horizon. I didn't know how my plans would change. I didn't know how much my dreams would change. I had no idea how much *I* was about to change. I had attended the same private school since kindergarten, so coming to a new school for the first time since the age of five felt like what I imagined a baby feels when it's being born: eyes open, limbs flailing. For me, coming to college was like wiggling all my toes for the first time. I was breaking free from a cocoon. The chance to reinvent myself felt like a second chance at life, so I threw myself in. I wanted to meet everyone. I wanted to do everything. I ran around campus like a mutant chicken whose head could be cut off and regrow, only to be instantly cut off again. To say I became a social butterfly would be a gross understatement. I was more like a social Mothra. I descended upon gatherings and events with monstrous force and appetite. Most nights, you could find me sprinting from dorm to dorm, ravenous for friendship, approval, and applause.

Unsurprisingly, shenanigans ensued. Milk challenges, late-night video-game competitions, water ballooning the student body from atop a nearby roof—you know, normal college stuff. Pranks happen, right? My friends Matt and DJ would go door to door with a cup of water and a bag full of baking flour. When a door would open to their gentle rapping, my buddies would toss the aforementioned substances in the faces of their victims and scream, "Shake 'n Bake!" It was hilarious—until it happened to you. There were last-minute road trips, late-night Slurpee runs, Top Ramen–eating competitions. My first semester was incredible. For a nineteen-year-old addicted to social validation, it was a perpetual high, and I had no interest in coming down.

I suppose I would have gone on this way a great deal longer if what happened next hadn't happened. But it did happen. (That's a lot of happens.) I encountered the Spirit of God. *Whoa, whoa whoa,* you might be thinking as you read this. *Let's just rein it in there, Mike. I didn't pick up this book to go all snake handling and drinking poison!* I get it. It seems like a weird thing to say. It's weirder still when I try to recount it.

One night as I was getting ready for a late-night PlayStation battle featuring *Tony Hawk's Pro-Skater,* I heard voices. Not in my head. I heard actual voices. They were singing. Quite confused, I began tearing around my dorm room like a madman with a metal detector. *Where on earth is that coming from?* I thought to myself. I pressed my ear up to the walls and staggered toward the door. I followed the voices out onto my hall's outdoor balcony on the fourth floor. I looked over the edge and found the source. A group of students was sitting in a little stone alcove in the courtyard of my dormitory. Some dudes with goatees were strumming a few acoustic guitars, accompanied by more good-looking girls than I could ever remember seeing in one place at the same time. I instinctively grabbed my guitar and hurtled down the stairway to join the choir.

I'll be completely honest here. I didn't go to sing. I went to meet those girls. I don't recall having a single overtly spiritual thought as I stumbled into my seat at the impromptu worship service. I thought this was going to be another makeshift karaoke session like singing around the campfire in high school. I only knew how to play four chords remotely well at the time, but I was ready to make the ladies swoon. Unbeknownst to me, there were greater forces than animal magnetism at work. Instead of acquiring the admiring gaze of the aforementioned females, I found I was the one gazing. I stared at these kids as if they had lobsters crawling from their ears, because I'd never witnessed anything like it before. I was perplexed. This was the first group of collegiate students who had freely chosen to come together and lift their attention heavenward. I had been a part of some makeshift Bible studies and whatnot before, but nothing like this.

Almost everyone in the circle had their eyes shut. No one was glancing around for approval. No one was looking around at all. Tears streamed freely down cheeks. I wondered what was making everyone so sad, but they weren't crying from sadness. Tears of joy flowed, faces tilted upward, and no one was paying any attention to me. Looking back, I'm surprised I stayed. For a kid who needed other people's approval so hungrily, it's strange I would be content to sit there unnoticed. But I did. I sat there and clumsily mimicked the guitar strumming of the players and took it all in. That night, I experienced another shift.

I remember walking back to my dorm room in a haze. Inexplicably, I wasn't thinking about girls anymore. I wasn't thinking about being seen anymore. I wasn't thinking about myself at all. It felt a lot like freedom. I didn't exactly know what happened that night, but I knew I needed it. So I went back for more. We began meeting every week. It was rarely planned. It wasn't organized, and from a strictly sonic perspective, it probably wasn't any good either. There were no sound systems or screens. No buildings or service times. All we had were our aching hearts and the need to be satisfied. Week after week, we would find one another down there in the tiny amphitheater at the bottom of Rinker Hall. Someone would read from the Bible, and then someone else would ask for prayer. Unscripted and spontaneous, it was unlike anything I had ever encountered. All these kids, who could have been out partying until they passed out, had gotten a taste of something better. So there they sat, and I along with them. We taught one another how to be captivated by the presence of God. We prayed. We sang. We were filled.

It changed me.

When I first arrived at school, all I wanted was to be famous. I had no idea what deep desires were really at play. All I knew was I needed to be seen. But by the end of my freshman year, after countless impromptu worship sessions, I became less obsessed with being seen. Ever so subtly, I was growing in my desire to see. Funny, because I remember being annoyed the first night. Every girl had her eyes closed so tight. I grumbled, "These girls are never gonna see me if they go on like that!"

But the truth was and still is, the more we look to the Father to fill us, the more capable we are of seeing the people right in front of us. We can stop seeing them for what they offer us and actually see others for what we can give them. Despite what contemporary culture might tempt us to believe, people aren't merely useful for pulling us up the social ladder. If we encounter Jesus, if we immerse our hearts in the reality of how He confronted social constructs during His time on earth, we just might see opportunities to follow His example and serve people as He did.

During this time, I met a kid named Jason who played the drums. He was really good, and since I was really not good at the guitar, I was simultaneously perplexed and aghast when a friend recommended we "jam together." Shockingly, Jason agreed. A few weeks later, we played at a battle of the bands together, and the following year, a local church asked us to do the music for a Wednesday night youth group. I've often told aspiring musicians and artists how crucial my freshman year was. It was in the midst of enjoying God for God alone that I began to grow in what we commonly refer to as *worship leading*. I like to call it *worship facilitating*. (I'll talk more about the *L* word later.) I truly believe that if I hadn't spent this simple time worshipping God for Himself, I would never have become any good at helping others worship Him.

Oftentimes, I've found that youth group worship teams work like this: Let's say you're an up-and-coming youth pastor and you look up one day to find you've got quite a few kids meeting at your weekly service. Now, you can't have a proper youth group without a youth band, right? So you begin to scour the group for anybody who is somewhat proficient at playing an instrument. Praise the Lord, there happens to be one kid who's not entirely horrible at the guitar, so you sign that kid up to be the "worship leader." The kid doesn't really know anything about God, or even what it means to follow Jesus, and he or she may have the spiritual proclivity of a donut. But this individual loves playing songs and definitely loves the attention that comes as a result.

Over time this kid you've chosen begins to wear the spiritual title of worship leader, and what's not to love? Everyone looks up to worship leaders. Everyone knows their names. They love being viewed as spiritually astute. Who wouldn't? But all the while they may never have actually experienced the love and validation from God they need to bring to the people. It's quite logical when you think about it.

It's also easy to imagine that they become too busy using people for the love and validation they've never received from God Himself. Here's the thing: I'm not saying everyone needs to sit around for hours singing "Kumbaya." I'm also not saying every youth group works in this way. I've met many young worshippers who were not only in love with their instrument but also deeply in love with Jesus. But what I am saying is that until you learn to worship God with no agenda or ulterior motive, there's a risk you'll end up using God to get something else. I like to call it "capitalistic Christianity." It's where we come to God with an expectation of a return on investment. "Okay, God, I'm gonna give you my obedience here, but I'd better get a return for it!"

When we start thinking of how little we can put in while keeping tabs on how much God owes us, things start to go sideways. For me it was an attempt to get noticed. I wanted to worship Him as long as it assured me the reputation of being "the guy who leads worship." I didn't realize then that accepting God's grace means He doesn't owe me anything anymore. If all I got from worshipping God was more of Him, that was more than enough. It took me a long time to wrap my head around, but now I'm certain Jesus offers us an acceptance we can come to the stage with, not go to the stage for. I know this, because no one would accept me when I started.

Not being good enough to lead worship was the best thing that ever happened to me. Even writing that sentence makes me laugh. It's so true. My freshman year of college, I tried to "lead" worship at school-sanctioned events, but I was shut down. I volunteered to play for the chapel praise team, but I was rejected. I simply wasn't good enough, having only started playing guitar a year before. There were plenty of other better players to choose from. Getting rejected was absolutely the best thing for me. I never would have admitted that at the time, mind you, because rejection never feels good when it's happening. However, I really believe if I had been thrown onstage any earlier, I might still be using the stage instead of being used on it.

The Second Applause

Let me confess something. Stepping onstage is still an intense struggle. When I'm on tour, I am onstage up to four or five times a week for months. Then you know what happens? I'll get applauded for simply showing up to work! And that, my friend, is dangerous. It's very, very dangerous. Postal workers rarely have to contend with this. No one I know is standing by their mailbox chanting, "Jim! Jim! Jim! My mail is here because of JIIMMM!"

Every single day, I have to check my ego at the door and figure out how to keep the applause from filling the spaces in my heart that the Spirit was meant to fill. My friend Al calls it "believing the second applause." Al should know. He has spent the last thirty years of his life counseling musicians and entertainers. To say he's heard it all would be a comical undersell. At a banquet for a group of musicians, Al explained the difference in applause. He said something to this effect:

> You should be clapped for and celebrated when you write
> songs or play an instrument incredibly. God did for Him-
> self, after all. On each day of creation, after staring at the
> blank page of nothingness, He sang all that is into its proper
> form. He gave the chaos function. And after each day, God
> stepped back from His work and said, "It is good." There's
> no danger in that. It's right. It's good. We ought to applaud
> what is created well, because God applauded Himself. The
> danger comes when we believe the second applause. The
> second applause is a quiet applause. It's the applause in

someone's mind that says, "Oh, he must be so amazing to have written that. That singer . . . he or she must be so incredible to be able to sing that way. She's in a class all her own. Oh, that guy must be far more spiritual than the rest of us to speak so clearly about God!"

Essentially, listening to the second applause is like believing your own hype. It's using your gifting to gain approval for yourself, instead of operating in your gifting from God's approval for the benefit of others.

Have you heard the Ben Rector song "The Men That Drive Me Places"? Not gonna lie; it's a weird title until you listen to it. Essentially, Ben is telling the stories of different taxi drivers he's had. He talks about the sacrifices they made and are making and how one guy has been working several jobs to help put his daughter through school. Just before the first chorus, Ben slips in this line, "And somehow I'm the one you people pay to see." The chorus continues, "Oh, how am I the only one who knows I'm half the man of the men that drive me places?"[1] When I first heard this song, I didn't make it through the chorus without crying. (I have four daughters. I'm a softie.) I cried because this is the gospel-saturated grateful heart's cry. It's a recognition that all we've been given is a gift and we're to see the rest of the world as though we've been dealt the best hand. Who are we to take the credit? Who are we to live from any place other than wonder and awe that we should get to do whatever it is we've been equipped to do. But when you listen too long to the second applause, you begin to believe you deserve it.

Don't Live for God

I'll never forget the time we played worship music for a state youth convention. This was several years after college, and our little band had a van and trailer by that time. Most of the time we set up our own speakers and lights, so we were kind of a one-stop shop for youth conferences. They could book the band and get production thrown in. We would get referrals from one youth convention to the next, and we were usually the in-house worship team for the week or weekend. Up to that point, the largest conference we'd ever done was for maybe three or four hundred students, I think, so this was a big step up. Thousands of people were packed into a hotel conference room, and we were kind of freaking out at the opportunity.

The theme of the week was "Live Big for God." I remember it distinctly because the kids were coerced into chanting it at the start of every session. It reminded me of the scene in the first *The Mummy* movie, when all the throngs were brainlessly repeating, "Imhotep! Imhotep!" The phrase "Live Big for God" kept running through my mind even when I went to sleep at night. But something about it didn't sit quite right with me. My stomach churned. I felt like I should say something but didn't want to undermine the team that brought us in. I wasn't exactly sure what was perplexing my spirit about it until the last morning, when I finally felt compelled to address it. I sheepishly introduced a song by saying, "I don't think you should live big for God." There was a collective gasp and a few very long moments of awkward silence. I strummed nervously on my guitar to gather my thoughts. "I don't think you should live big for God until you learn how to live because of God." The whole crowd exhaled in relief. I summed up my position by saying, "Living for God is only possible because of all God has done for us. Don't try to serve Him until you are deeply in awe of how He's served you." Maybe it doesn't seem like a big distinction, but for me, it's been paramount.

It's a striking transformation to stand onstage and look out at a crowd and not feel like I necessarily have to do anything *for* them or *for* God. It's a whole different kind of freedom to stand up there and approach a microphone, simply because I am loved and I want to remind others of their belovedness. It feels less like an invest-and-reward paradigm and more like a service. I truly believe every believer, whether they are applauded for their contribution or not, ought to view their work as service. I like this visual. Unless you view the microphone as a toilet brush, you have no business holding it so tight. Unless I approach a microphone the way a janitor takes up his mop, chances are I won't be singing songs to serve others; I'll be singing so others serve me. If you serve or work merely for what you're going to get, or for how much you're going to do for God because of it, then you're constantly going to be keeping a mental tally in your head. Were you applauded enough? Were you recognized adequately for all you've accomplished? Chances are you'll end up feeling slighted. Inevitably, there will come a time when you feel you deserve better than what you're getting. But when all you do is because of God, there's no more deserving. There's only grace.

These ideas started to take shape a few years before the conference while I was still learning my craft in college. My junior year, my drummer friend, Jason, and I had been facilitating worship at a local church for over a year. Bryan, Jason's future brother-in-law (though he didn't know that yet), played bass, and our newfound friend, Drew, was playing electric guitar and singing too. Drew looked kind of like Skeeter from the old cartoon show *Doug*. He also had a facial expression that made him look like he was mad at you. We were constantly asking him, "Are you okay?" He would immediately smile and say, "Yeah, of course! Why? Was my face looking angry? I'm sorry. I'm Russian. I have an angry resting face." You don't really need to know that. I just think it's funny.

Whether we liked it or not, the majority of the large youth group held our little worship band in high esteem. They even created some awkward tension between the local Christian radio station and us. So many kids from the youth group would call in requesting our music that the station actually contacted us and asked us to make them stop. They told us, "We will not now or ever play your music!" We understood their response because those kids were relentless.

I seriously have never felt more famous than when I was onstage every Wednesday night at my local church. I ran into people everywhere who knew who I was. I'd hear my name at the local Starbucks, and then someone would pat me on the back and say, "Good worship last week, bro!" We started getting asked to play at birthday parties on the weekend. It was weird. More than once, some girl's mom would find me after a service and put her hand on my shoulder, saying, "How old are you? Because my daughter goes to the youth group . . ." Seriously awkward. And like I said, dangerous. Slowly I began seeing myself as more valuable than everyone else. When a lot of people know your name, it's easy to believe your name is worth more than theirs.

Often I would find a line forming near the stage at the end of the Wednesday night service as I was packing up my guitar. Generally, the kids in line seemed to all be socially awkward and uncomfortable talking to other kids—or any other humans, for that matter. But that was just how it seemed.

At first, I handled it miserably. I was way too into my newfound Christian celebrity to be bothered by such minions. I would leave before anyone could talk to me, looking right over their shoulders to flag down one of the college girls who was helping. After all, I was a big deal, right? I was a leader! Did they not know how much I had on my plate? I was doing too much for God to waste my precious time on some measly high schoolers! Thankfully, though, those early days of sitting in a circle and learning to treasure God flashed back in my mind and made their way to my heart. I recalled that not so long before, I too was desperate to be seen. I too needed someone's steady gaze to feel my worth. Truth be told, I still did. I still do. So I made a commitment one Wednesday night: "I'm going to look each of these kids in the eyes and talk to them until they're done. Even if I have to shut the building down, even if I'm the last one there, I'm going to give everything I have to them." My capitalistic Christianity was slowly unraveling.

God Didn't Invest in Me

I know this is going to take some unlearning for most of us. It did for me. I grew up in a capitalistic society—one that glorified the ethos "the least amount of investment for the greatest amount of return." That's great for business ventures, but it's absolutely toxic when it affects how we view God and, consequently, how we treat people. Dietrich Bonhoeffer said, "We must learn to regard people less in the light of what they do or omit to do, and more in the light of what they suffer."[2]

I'd like to add, we must learn to regard people more in light of how we can bless them and less for what they can do for us. Grace was never meant to be a business plan. The gospel works on an entirely different paradigm. We're not in a capitalistic relationship with Jesus. I heard a teacher named Steve Guthrie say, "God does not come to us demanding payment. He comes to us offering payment." You could argue that Jesus gave the greatest amount of investment for the least amount of return. The King of heaven can't ever get something in return that's better than what He's already given, and yet He joyfully gives everything to be in relationship with you and me.

Unbelievable.

It's helpful to remind ourselves that God's not an investment banker. He didn't save us because He needed help on His return. This changes the way we see ourselves. It unravels the law of averages and all the other ways we tend to try to quantify our relationship with God. In college, I was taught how important a steady return on investment was. Through Myspace and Facebook, I learned I could garner great returns on very little social investment. When I could be receiving a hundred comments from a post that took five seconds to write, talking to people eye to eye seemed like an extravagant waste of time. I already had a hard enough time thinking about other people, but when the digital reformation hit, it was game over. Currently, it doesn't take more than a glance around a busy airport to see how much we are defined by the Latin phrase *incurvatus in se,* meaning, "curved in on ourselves."[3] Eyes down. Heads down. It's easier than ever to disengage from the world around us because we engage with the world we create. I know, I know. We're not narcissistic, you might argue. We're just efficient! We're getting things done. We're being more productive! We're expanding our reach and influence! I'm sure we are. But there are always two sides to the story. If we're doing so much for other people in our digital cages, why do we consult our news feeds a hundred times a day to see what people are saying about us? Or am I the only one who struggles with that?

At the end of the day, God will always invest far more in us than we'll ever be able to return to Him. Whew. Let that truth wash over you for just a minute. I know it's hard. With all our curated feeds and hand-selected friendships, it's almost impossible to accept grace like that. We were a particularly poor investment for Jesus. Yet that didn't stop Him from pouring His life out for us. He didn't love us for what we'd be able to give back. He loves us because He is love. Our lack of reciprocation doesn't stop Him from pouring His Spirit into us. Therefore, shouldn't we offer ourselves to those around us in the same way?

To find God's life for our will, we must become well acquainted with the truth that capitalism is not the same thing as Christianity. With any due diligence, you'll find that they are diametrically opposed. The way of Jesus does not resemble a stock market graph with perpetual gains. It looks more like a series of joyful losses. Yes, you read that correctly. In God's kingdom, even losses are a chance for joy. We already have all we need, so whatever we lose we give up freely. Like Him, we lay down even our own lives. They are not taken from us. His example allows us to willingly waste ourselves on others. I know. It doesn't sound very efficient, does it? But the hard truth is, grace won't work any other way. God isn't efficient. Why else would He use us?

It happened too. Almost every Wednesday, after I committed to being there as long as those kids wanted to talk, my will was changed. I often found myself in the parking lot after all the lights were off in the church. The youth pastor was already locking up the front doors, and there were still three or four more kids waiting to tell their troubles to someone who would listen. In the world's economy, they didn't have anything to offer me, but I had time, and so I offered what I could to them. Slowly, steadily, I began to see how wrong I was too. They had far more to offer me than I had first realized. They were, one at a time, helping to give me the ability to see people as Jesus saw them. I can't think of a better thing to be able to offer. Eventually, their parents would come and pick them up. Sometimes I would end up driving a carload of kids home, but it was worth it. I couldn't see it at the time, but the simple act of opening my eyes to the people in front of me helped secure in my heart how Jesus looked at me.

The Ministry
of Interruption

The truth is of course that what one
calls the interruptions are precisely
one's real life—the life God is sending
one day by day.

—C. S. LEWIS

At another youth conference, around the same time as the "Live Big for God" conference, I met a pastor named Chuck. Chuck pastors a church in Portland, Oregon. I knew I liked him from the start. Once he said to me in passing, "Yeah, I'm praying God doesn't grow my church right now, because we don't have enough laypeople to effectively disciple people." Chuck sees things differently. He recognizes he isn't here to build his own private kingdom; he's part of a much bigger one.

Among other things, I also credit Chuck with helping me get married. When I expressed to him all those reasons I wasn't sure I should marry my girlfriend, Chuck quipped, "Wow. Sounds like your problem is you have an American view of marriage." Not only does Chuck see things for what they are, but he also says what he sees.

"How do you figure?" I shot back.

"Well, looks like you're worried you won't find a woman who gives you everything you want while demanding nothing from you. Marriage doesn't work like that."

"Dang it, Chuck. You're making me feel quite uncomfortable."

"Good," he responded with a wry smile.

On the second night of the first conference we did together, Chuck spoke to the kids about one person in the Bible who was transformed by how Jesus looked at him. It wrecked me so hard, I remember going up to my room and weeping on my balcony for two hours. I was sure I had never allowed myself to be seen with God's eyes.

In Mark 7:31–37, we read about a group of friends who brought a deaf and mute man to the Lord and pleaded with Him to do something. In that culture, physical disability was widely believed to be the result of some sin in you or in your family line. You were getting what you deserved. Naturally, you were then looked down on as lower than the rest of society. In some cases, you weren't even seen as fully human. It's important to understand that perspective to grasp how shocking Jesus's response truly was. Instead of being repulsed or being too caught up in His own agenda, Jesus chose not to cast this man aside. Nope. Jesus held him. He didn't just hold him either. He held him by the face. He looked him dead in the eye and saw the man the crowds couldn't. Jesus treated this man like royalty, not refuse.

Just to humanize him further, let's call the man Ralph. After leading Ralph and his friends away from the crowds, Jesus put His fingers in Ralph's ears. Ralph was probably taken aback and maybe even fearful at that point. I imagine that if Jesus put His fingers in Ralph's ears, He would have had to put His palms on Ralph's face. I can't even imagine what Ralph was thinking. The next bit is even crazier. Jesus spit and then touched Ralph's tongue. I'm guessing Ralph was pretty grossed out, maybe even trembling at this point. I mean, what's scarier than crazy, right? But then it happened. Jesus whispered, "Ephphatha," and Ralph's mouth dropped open because, for the first time, he heard it. His ears were opened. He began to speak. I wonder how many tears fell on Jesus as the group embraced. And I wonder how many opportunities I have missed because the "Ralphs" of the world didn't look like they had much to offer me.

Jesus in Disguise

I'll never forget the time I played basketball with an intellectually disabled boy. I didn't want to. No, seriously. When I asked him to play, I didn't know he was disabled. To this day, I still don't actually know what was technically wrong with him, but I did find out what was wrong with me.

In January of 2011, I was on a large music tour called Winter

Jam. We were traveling through most of the United States, playing forty-seven shows. I'm pretty sure it was forty-seven. It was definitely forty-seven . . . or something close. The particular fun of this tour was the number of artists on it. I think there were ten different groups altogether. Think of it as a touring festival, or even a moving summer camp, depending on how you look at it. For a bunch of touring musicians who frequently are traveling on their own for months on end, it was a welcome respite to have a family atmosphere for a few months.

After the first couple of weeks of the tour, a group of about twelve of us really got into playing basketball. We'd find a local YMCA and converge there around one o'clock every afternoon. It may not sound like a big deal to you, but to those of us who had been cooped up backstage or on the road for months on end, those two hours of cardio activity were like Christmas. After a month or so into the tour, we had a great rhythm going. We usually had enough guys to play full court, and we seized every opportunity we had. One day, we gathered at the gym and realized we were a player short. We had only nine and were beginning to decide who would sit out, when I spotted a guy by himself on the other end of the gym. Before I realized what I was doing, I yelled, "Hey, man! We need one more! You want to play?"

When the dude turned and screamed "YEEAAAH!," I could hear the collective groan of disappointment from the entire group. Now, no one would ever own up to being frustrated. But I'm not trying to make us look good here; I'm trying to be gut-level honest. In that moment when I realized what I had initiated, I didn't want to inconvenience myself. I would love to lie to you and say I embraced the opportunity, but sadly, I was much more concerned with myself and having a good time. I didn't want to be some kid's babysitter. Grudgingly, we started playing.

As soon as this kid touched the ball, he threw up the worst-looking shot I have ever seen in my life. The ball hung in the air for an impossible amount of time. I'm not joking. I think I retied both of my shoes while it made its way to the basket. We all stopped and watched its flight. It arched up and up, until it nearly clipped the roof of the gym. Then our mouths collectively dropped open when the ball finally finished its descent by finding its intended destiny. *Swish*. Nothing but net. We all just stood there and stared in disbelief. The kid was already running down the court pumping his fist like he'd won the NBA Finals. We shrugged it off as one bright flash of serendipity, and normal play commenced.

The other team missed a shot, and we brought it back down the court. We passed it around a couple of times, and then, again, as soon as the new kid touched the ball, he heaved up another desperation toss. I'm pretty sure this one did actually skim the rafters sixty feet up before it came down and—you guessed it—nothing but net.

Now everyone was smiling. Both his arms were high above his head, and he screamed in unparalleled euphoria. Third time down. You can probably guess where this is going. He got the ball, this time from well behind the three-point line, and before we could blink, another awkward heave careened through the universe until it came splashing down for his third straight bucket.

This time, there were tears. I'm not kidding. Some of the guys were laughing. Some were actually crying tears of joy. Most of us were hugging. Everyone was high-fiving. Everyone. The game finally picked back up after a good five-minute celebration, and this kid probably played for another twenty minutes before he had to go. He threw up plenty more shots—none of which, I might add, came anywhere close to going in. In fact, several went over the backboard and out of the gym. But it didn't matter. God, it would seem, had made His point. By means of what felt like interruption, we found a miracle waiting for us. The great miracle, of course, was coming to terms with my own self-centeredness. I quickly came face to face with the realization that I had been missing out by just living for myself. How many divine moments had I missed in my life, simply because I was too determined to live for my own agenda?

This, of course, should come as no great surprise, because it's exactly how Jesus did ministry. He loved without agenda. He never missed what the Father had prepared for Him, no matter how the opportunity disguised itself. Jesus always embraced the ministry of interruption.

Jesus Interrupted

Jesus did far more than take a few minutes out of His day to play basketball with someone. It's actually kind of embarrassing to admit I didn't jump at the opportunity to bless when it was presented to me. I didn't see it as a chance to host angels unaware (Hebrews 13:2). I didn't see what was right in front of me because I wanted to minister on my timetable. I was "ministering" every night onstage, so I couldn't be bothered when I wasn't in the mind-set, could I? Of course, I've come to realize now, I missed what was right in front of me because most ministry opportunities have a way of disguising themselves as inconveniences.

I love how 1 Peter 3:9 reads in The Message, "No retaliation. No sharp-tongued sarcasm. Instead, bless—that's your job, to bless. You'll be a blessing and also get a blessing." What would my life look like if I filtered every moment through that simple instruction? Jesus always blessed, didn't He? Everywhere He went. Everyone He met. He blessed. He never seemed to be repulsed. He never seemed to stop and weigh out the risk versus reward on His investments. Lepers, prostitutes, the poor, the sick, hypocrites, even the Pharisees—Jesus was never deterred by weakness; it was almost as if He was attracted to it. Yeah, I suppose He was, wasn't He? He was so attracted to our weaknesses that He came to earth to heal them.

What's really interesting to me is how we want to be like Jesus in this way but feel like we need to choose a team. For instance, I've heard people read about Jesus and say, "See, He was hanging out with the drunks and the prostitutes, so we shouldn't be hanging out with religious people!" I agree on one hand because Jesus absolutely hung out with all kinds of social riffraff, but He also hung out with the Pharisees. What's amazing about Jesus's ministry was how insanely unbiased it was. Just when you think He was really making a splash in the synagogue, extrapolating truths with the spiritual elite, He went and healed a man on the Sabbath and angered the religious elites. He then upset the marginalized by having dinner at a Pharisee's house. It was almost as if Jesus was perpetually shooting Himself in the foot. If you're going to succeed on a social level, you need to align yourself with a particular demographic, right? But I don't think that's what He was doing. I think Jesus was just intent on investing in every kind of person, no matter the kickback.

Do you remember the story about Jairus's daughter in Mark 5? Jairus was a high-ranking official in a local synagogue, and his daughter grew ill. He sought out Jesus and asked Him to come heal her. Jesus agreed to go see Jairus's daughter. I imagine the disciples celebrated this news. "Yes!" they must have whispered back and forth. "This is the big leagues! This Jairus guy is a big deal! If Jesus heals his daughter, this ministry is really going to grow! Think of the influence we'll gain! Roman Empire, here we come!"

But notoriety wasn't on Jesus's radar, nor was He interested in being a political poster child. The next thing you know, Jesus was walking through a crowd on His way to Jairus's house when a woman who had been bleeding for twelve years grabbed hold of Jesus's robe from behind and was healed. Jesus's reaction is truly incredible:

> Jesus, perceiving in himself that power had gone out from
> him, immediately turned about in the crowd and said,
> "Who touched my garments?" And his disciples said to
> him, "You see the crowd pressing around you, and yet
> you say, 'Who touched me?'" And he looked around to
> see who had done it. But the woman, knowing what had
> happened to her, came in fear and trembling and fell down
> before him and told him the whole truth. And he said to

her, "Daughter, your faith has made you well; go in peace, and be healed of your disease." (Mark 5:30–34)

First off, you have to remember the time and culture in which Jesus lived to really appreciate what's happening here. In that society, simply being a woman meant you were less important and less powerful than a man was. In addition, women were considered unclean during their monthly menstrual cycle, so this woman was probably shunned. Another rabbi might have tried to pretend he didn't notice her, since he would have run the risk of becoming unclean himself by touching her. At the very least, Jesus would have been required by Jewish law to cleanse himself after being touched by her. But that didn't seem to matter to Him. Jesus did the unthinkable. He stopped and blessed her.

The disciples must have been losing their minds. "What are You doing, Jesus? Who touched You? WHO CARES? We have a schedule to keep! There's an official's daughter to heal! You're wasting precious time!"

But Jesus saw what they couldn't. He bent low. He spoke to the woman. What's even more baffling about His actions is that she had already been healed. I believe that simply by stopping, Jesus was trying to tell the disciples something. He was taking a sacred moment to communicate to her what we all need to hear: *I see you. I love you. You're not a waste of My time.*

The next moment, Jairus's servants showed up and confirmed that the little girl was dead. The opportunity had been squandered. "Relax," Jesus encouraged them. "She's only sleeping." He went on to bring this little girl back to life, and in doing so, He reminds all of us to open our eyes to every person, every moment. "Whatever you did for one of the least of these . . . you did for me," Jesus reminds us in the book of Matthew.[1] As Mother Teresa surmised, Jesus often wears distressing disguises.[2] She also lived her life by this motto: "We can do no great things. Just small things, with great love."[3] This helps me greatly. Even the people who used to look like an enormous waste of my time now look like the very face of God.

Declassifying People

One of the surest ways I can follow Jesus's example is to constantly work against my natural tendency to classify people in social interactions. When I flip on the news, it's quickly apparent we believe in demons and heroes and there really isn't much room in between. We love to talk about *them* or *those people* when discussing politics or religion or fill-in-the-blank. But I think what a Christian should bring to the world is the belief that our enemy is not a person or group of people. Our enemy isn't flesh and blood; it's the "spiritual forces of evil" (Ephesians 6:12, NIV). Our enemy is sin. Our enemy is hatred. So we must fight against anything in our own hearts that would hinder a spirit of reconciliation. We don't have to be right, but we are commanded to love. Anchored by the truth of the gospel, we believe that people are more than what they do. If Jesus's work for us becomes our new identity, then we begin to see others through the same lens.

I live in Nashville now. I've lived here since the fall of 2008. I love it. It has a beautiful small-town feel combined with a big-city vibe that's unlike anywhere else I've been. There are tons of local restaurants and everyone is an artist. Whether they're into music or donut making, people create amazing things here with a fantastic amount of care and attention to detail. It is of course a music town. Some might argue it's *the* music town. With that comes an astonishing level of mastery, but it also comes with some natural social idiosyncrasies.

The great part for me about living in a town full of musicians is that there's a level of camaraderie and understanding. We know what it's like sleeping on a bus or doing sound check or what have you. We get one another, so we don't have to explain ourselves and we can move on to talking about life. The awkward thing about living in a music town is that "knowing the right people" can quickly become a full-time job. Regardless of where you live, I'm sure you've experienced that. It probably is just elevated in a town where your occupation hinges on who you've met, what you've accomplished, and who you know. We've all been at a party or some kind of event where we've been the victim of a "too unimportant to keep talking to" moment. You know, you're in the middle of a conversation, and you see the eyes of the person you're talking to slowly scan the room over your shoulder. It doesn't take a genius to surmise where you stand on the social credibility ladder in that setting. "Excuse me," I want to say, "I'm right here."

What if Jesus wants us to break that cycle? What if we acted like no one was beneath us? What if I could enter a social setting ready to give worth rather than trying to garner it? What if I didn't need to meet the most famous person in the room? And not just so I could be the cool guy in the room who isn't "impressed" by famous people. What if I wasn't friends with you because of what you could do for my career? What if I was as wasteful with my time as Jesus? He loved the unfamous, the famous, and the infamous alike.

This approach is not popular. Once I entered my thirties, it seemed like people stopped being people. In work environments, we started to call them fans, followers, or customers. We don't even see ourselves as people, because we're too consumed with branding ourselves. We curate the life right out of our friendships. The advice we used to offer freely to the people around us is now expertise sold at a premium. The other day I had lunch with a friend, and he was encouraging me to charge people thousands of dollars to "life coach" them. I looked up from my salad confused. "Life coach?" I slowly chewed over my kale (I'm so healthy) and those words.

"I think that's just a more profitable word for friend, right?"

The thought stayed with me. I don't want to be anyone's coach; I want to be their friend. If I have to miss capitalistic experiences, so be it. This famous idiom rings true: "We make a living by what we get, but we make a life by what we give."[4] After all, I'd rather have loved ones speaking at my funeral than be buried in a really expensive coffin.

The Leader Label Lie

No man can be a good bishop if he loves
his title but not his task.

—SAINT AUGUSTINE, THE CITY OF GOD

Names. We respond to them. We are known by them. They have the power to call us out, to crush us, or set us free. The names we are given and the names we take can influence who we believe we are and who we're meant to be. I never thought much about my name until I was sixteen and got a job at Einstein Bros. Bagels. For the first time I realized just how much power a name and a name tag could give. Several of my friends had taken jobs there, so they naturally recruited me to leave my illustrious employment with Hollywood Video and join their ranks as a bagel purveyor. As my boss began outlining the dress code my first day on the job, I thought I had died and gone to bagel heaven. A company T-shirt, tennis shoes, a hat of our choosing, and a name tag was all that was demanded. The name tag, he explained, we were to create for ourselves. To help you understand my glee, I should tell you that while working at Hollywood Video, I had been forced to wear a tuxedo shirt, cummerbund, and bow tie. So the laid-back change in apparel was one I was eager to make. Before taking up my position at the Einstein's register, I eagerly snatched up a small piece of white cardboard and began to write my name.

The thought hit me. Wait a second. I could write anything I wanted. I could be anyone I wanted. I could call myself Stewart or Francois. I could be Jamal or Bartholomew. Wow. The possibilities were endless. There was nothing in the company rulebook that required employees to use their given birth names. I felt it was my duty to exploit this loophole. What would I write? Who would I be? After a meticulous five-minute deliberation with myself, I decided on Morgan. It's my middle name and the name I sometimes wish my parents had actually named me. Michael is great. It means "Who is like the Lord?" Which I love, because it's a question, and I love questions. But it's annoying when they call out "Mike" for tacos or something and ten dudes come up for the order. As a type four on the Enneagram, I decided that Morgan was the obvious choice since Michael felt far less mysterious. For the first two months I worked there, I made a new name tag every day. I always wrote down "MORGAN." Usually all caps and with plenty of stars and confetti. Sometimes I'd draw flying dogs or whatever else came into my mind. At sixteen, having strangers call me by my middle name felt unusually exhilarating. I know it sounds dumb, but I felt empowered. Suddenly, the future felt broader. I was unboxed, in a way. I could be more than the labels I had acquired to that point.

I had no idea how true this would be for the rest of my life. We all are after a bit of power and excitement by how others view us, aren't we? In a sense, our whole lives long, we're all back in the break room of the bagel shop, scribbling down a name we want to be known by. Will it be a name that suggests mystery or demands respect? Will we go for one that denotes strength or one that inspires creativity? Will we choose a name that frees us or enslaves us? That might sound dramatic, but the names we wear can dictate the motivations we live by.

It happened again this past weekend. I was out on tour and wanted to plop down at a local coffee shop for a couple of hours. The tour manager said the runner was waiting out in the van and was ready to take me. I grabbed my bag from the bus and jumped in with a stranger. Very quickly, I found myself neck deep in the name-game conversation with the driver. It was the same conversation I've had countless times since I began having customers call me Morgan.

My driver's name was Bradford. He seemed embarrassed when he said it. "I was going to be Desiree if I was a girl. I don't know where my mom got the name Bradford. I think the doctor had something to do with it."

I thought it was an awesome name. I immediately made a reference to John Bradford and how he is quoted as saying, "There, but for the grace of God, goes John Bradford."

I added, "I love that perspective. We tend to label ourselves as better than others, but John Bradford realized that the prisoners of whom he spoke those words, the ones who were supposedly being led to their execution, could have been him if it weren't for the undeserved grace of God in his life. Isn't that an amazing mind-set?"

I looked over and waited for a response. Bradford was unimpressed. "So you like to read, huh?" he said.

"Yeah," I answered. "It's a pretty amazing thing to have the power of information at your fingertips, don't you think?"

"I guess so," Bradford answered. "I like audio books."

"Oh nice," I said. "What books have you listened to lately?"

"Oh, you know . . ." I noticed he bit his bottom lip, trying to think of titles while simultaneously merging onto the interstate. "Leadership books mainly. I'm just trying to learn how to be successful."

I probed at this. "Oh, of course. So, what would success look like in your mind, if you don't mind my asking?"

I could tell Bradford was beginning to feel equal parts shocked, honored, and concerned that I was going so deep so quickly. "You know, man . . . not having to worry about money."

"What else?" I stabbed one last time.

"I guess I want to be thought of as a leader."

Bingo. There it was. We talked for a few more minutes and were just starting to lament the misuse of power in the current political environment when we arrived at the aforementioned caffeinating destination. I thanked him for the conversation, and he thanked me for "not being one of those artists who doesn't talk to people." I bought him a coffee, and we went our separate ways. A few minutes later, I sat down with my carefully crafted cortado and wondered when the label of "leader" seemingly became the end-all be-all for human existence.

Maybe you think I'm exaggerating, but when it comes to choosing one from all the million possibilities to write down on the dangling tag on our chests, I honestly can't tell you how many times I've heard the moniker "leader" emerge from someone's lips. It would seem the resounding ethos of the Western culture I live in carries the mandate "Don't be a follower. Be a trendsetter. Just do it. Lead. Lead. Lead." Those taglines go deeper than we realize. Quickly, and perhaps subconsciously, a culture's values blur into moral imperatives. We are constantly bombarded with the Canon marketing tagline that Andre Agassi made famous: "Image is everything."

John Bradford disagreed. In his mind, he was a prisoner who had been graciously set free. "There but for the grace of God goes John Bradford." A guy who says that isn't thinking, *Call me Leader.* He's got to be thinking, *Call me Redeemed.* Now that's a label that won't let you down. Like driver Bradford, I think you and I would do well to take a second and redefine what success is. What label is worth living for, and what label will end up living us? Some name badges might sound prestigious but make for shaky ground when we begin to build our identity on them.

Sadly, in my own life, I've settled for the company label instead of a name I can always count on. Why do I do that? Why do I settle for the mirage of pretense instead of insisting on being the wonderful and wild mystery God has made me to be? In chapter 2, I said the most important label I ever received was "child of God." For most of us, including myself, it's tempting to exchange that label because it's simply not impressive enough.

You know what name tag has really got me rolling lately? "Public figure." I'm sorry, I laugh every time I see that on a profile page. I imagine one of my bagel purveying coworkers writing that down on their little chest plate. "Well, of course you are." I think to myself. "Aren't we all?" I can only guess someone's intention for that title, but I have to think they're trying to convince everyone they are a person more in the public eye than normal humans are. They have the world's attention. Maybe they're just trying to convince themselves. I don't know for sure, but it feels like thin glass to walk on. A name that is dependent on perception is a name that's bound to break under your feet eventually. If your name is "public figure," what happens when the public isn't interested in you anymore? Do you even exist at that point? Sounds like a ton of unnecessary pressure to me.

Declassifying ourselves is harder than it sounds. It will demand that we stop demanding. For instance, to strip away the idea of being a public figure means the public no longer owes you their fascination. I heard the actor Jeff Goldblum say the key to being interesting is to be interested. As an actor, the minute you try to come across as interesting, you won't be. The key is to be deeply interested in whatever it is you're doing. To be fascinated is what leads to being fascinating. Letting go of the "leader" persona means nobody owes you their following. They're free to follow you or not. Turning your attention off yourself gives others the same freedom.

To me that sounds like an exhale of relief long overdue. And not only for us; letting others remain a mystery is freeing as well. Yes, it takes an incredible amount of energy. The other day I walked through the mall and tried empathizing deeply with every person I saw. It wore me out. I wanted to take a nap after ten minutes. It's so much easier to look at a Chick-fil-A employee as simply that, an employee. We rarely ask the baby-faced teen taking our order about the value meal while simultaneously remembering that he or she is an individual with a unique, complex life and story. This person had a fifth birthday. A first day of school. Possibly has just had a first kiss. Who knows? It's been my experience that every person is a Cracker Jack box full of surprises. If only we could truly keep our eyes off ourselves long enough to see them.

Listen, I get it. As I explained earlier, I worked at a church for seven years. During that time, I learned quickly how much easier it is to lump people together. When you look out at a couple thousand people from the stage, if you don't work at focusing on unique faces, you stop seeing the truth. You're tempted to identify the throng as nothing more than a crowd. My friend Jon has helped me in this area. Jon has played in a rock band for over twenty years, and he regularly tries to make eye contact with as many individuals as he can at each concert. This helps him remember that every crowd consists of individual people. It is still downright exhausting, though. It is for me now, and it was for me then. Working at a megachurch, I was looking at over ten thousand people bustling in and out of five services every weekend. Standing up on a stage, how could I not begin to think my name tag was more important than theirs—even though it wasn't?

Scratch the Leader Label

When I was on staff at the church, it was drilled into my head that I needed to embrace my new label as a leader in the corporation. The other staff members and I were told, "You are leaders. Everyone is looking to you as an example. You must be the kind of leaders God wants you to be."

I nodded vigorously. *Absolutely,* I thought. *I'm going to be so awesome at being awesome.* I was going to slap that "leader" name tag on and wear it proudly. No matter how flimsy it would turn out to be. Thankfully, one day I made a startling discovery. I had been searching the Gospels for it. I was combing through the pages of the Bible daily, examining commentaries and study versions. I kept thinking, *Surely today I'm going to find it. This is the day it's going to jump off the page.* But that day never came. I realized that Jesus never once asked someone to wear the name *leader*. Search for yourself. It isn't there. In the moment, I was offended; in time, I was relieved. It has since borne serious implications. If Jesus never asked anyone to lead, then maybe none of us should be trying to be known as leaders.

"Blasphemy!" you might exclaim. "Leadership is the most important of all character qualities! It ought to be the goal of every Christ follower!"

Should it? Have you ever stopped to ask why leadership isn't listed as part of the fruit of the Spirit in Galatians 5? Could it be that leadership is a human invention? Could it be that the longing to be known as a leader is really just lust for power? Isn't it essentially the same temptation Adam and Eve faced in the garden? We want to make the rules. We want to decide what is right and wrong. Could it be that we have latched on to the term *leader* simply because it helps us spiritualize our greed for control? Not to mention the fact that if Jesus was really asking us all to be leaders, who would be left to follow?

Maybe your thoughts go where mine did when I first started to ponder this. Maybe you recall all the times the New Testament talks about leaders of the church. I thought about that too. Turns out, every time you read the word *leader*, it would have been better translated from the original Greek as "overseer" or "shepherd." These roles are certainly not the same as our contemporary vision of a leader. We are usually thinking of the man or woman out front or onstage, the one who is really in charge. That's our idea of a leader.

You might ask, "But what about Peter? He was *the* leader of the church! Christ appointed Him, right?"

Absolutely. Jesus pulled Peter aside and told him, "You are Peter, and on this rock I will build my church" (Matthew 16:18, NIV).[1] But is that the same thing as asking him to be a leader? Notice that when Christ spoke to Peter on the beach after the resurrection, He didn't say, "Peter, lead my sheep." Instead, Jesus said, "Feed my sheep" (John 21:17). It might be good for us to pause and think of the posture it requires to bend low to feed an animal. Obviously Jesus is using this as an analogy for serving people, but the imagery has to be on purpose. Peter is told to serve others in the manner in which a shepherd feeds his quadrupeds. This is not what I'd consider a high-profile position.

As I continued my research into Jesus's interactions, I did not find any instances when He called people to be leaders. Whether it was the disciples, the rich young ruler, or others, His words to each were the same: "Come, and follow Me."

Follow.

Follow.

Follow.

Jesus doesn't seem to require leadership skills of anyone; He only bids them come and follow Him.

Obviously, you and I have no control over the labels given to us. If we take the initiative to help or guide others, people will start calling us leaders. This shouldn't change our focus. Our focus ought to remain fixed on who God is and who we are in light of His love. We must constantly resist the temptation to fixate on how others see us.

It's hard though, isn't it? Since the days of Constantine, the church has repeatedly given in to the temptation to gain power through its own efforts. We don't want to have to experience suffering, choose self-denial, or develop humility as Christ did. Being a servant isn't as cool or sexy as being a leader. I would argue that's why we have leadership conferences and not "followership" conferences. It's why leadership books outsell servanthood ones. Maybe servanthood doesn't need a conference because the Holy Spirit will always equip those who want to serve. Unfortunately, I think leadership will always be a marketable topic because it appeals to our egos.

I recently started debating this point with my friend Timothy. Our friendship goes back years, to when we did summer youth camps and weekend conferences together. As we were driving to the Baylor campus where Tim was leading a college ministry, he said, "So, let me get this straight. You're telling me I'm not supposed to be a leader?"

"Well, yes and no," I responded. "It's not that you shouldn't strive to facilitate well. If God has placed you in a position of authority over others, your job is to serve them. But that's my point. I don't think attaining the title of leader should be a personal goal. I think your goal should simply be to follow Jesus and serve the people He puts in your life as best you can. Leadership is not something that even needs to be on your radar."

He countered, "I pray this prayer for my two young boys every night: 'God, may my boys follow You and become great leaders of men.' What's wrong with that?"

"Well, nothing," I said. "It's just redundant. I'm saying you don't even need to be worried about the second part. Why couldn't you just pray that your boys would follow Jesus? Regardless of whether others see them as leaders or not, isn't that up to God? I don't know about you, but I want to reject any label other than 'child of God.' I've tried other labels, and they only weigh me down. I'm done trying to make a name for myself. I'm done trying to leave a legacy, and I'm done disguising my complacency as trust in God's sovereignty. I'm done impressing. I'm done with building my own reputation. And, yes, I'm even done trying to be a leader."

"Well, yeah. I think you have a point," Timothy conceded.

This, I think, is the point. I don't think there's anything wrong with others seeing you as a leader. I understand we need to know where the buck stops in a business or organization. If you're charismatic or personable, chances are others will start looking to you for cues. Whether we're at work, in a group, or at a party, we'll see some people exhibiting certain qualities and personality traits that cause the rest of us to defer to them. There's nothing inherently wrong with that. But I think a lot can go wrong for all of us when an individual seeks power or wants to be known as the leader. Do you want to lead by serving as Jesus did, or do you want to be labeled a leader while other people serve you?

Jesus didn't say to the disciples, "Follow me, and make yourselves fishers of men." Instead, He said, "Follow me, and I will make you fishers of men" (Matthew 4:19). Jesus didn't say, "Abide in me and go bear fruit." Rather, He said, "Whoever abides in me and I in him, he it is that bears much fruit" (John 15:5). You see, Jesus didn't focus on the results. He kept the main thing the main thing. He knew that if His only desire was to follow His Father's will, everything else would fall into place. I'll admit, I had to laugh as I wrote that, because even that looked so much different to Jesus from what it does to us. For Jesus, that involved dying on the cross and descending into hell. I'm sure this isn't what we envision as God's will for our lives. All but one of the disciples were martyred. I daresay that most of us taking notes in leadership conferences aren't hoping for that sort of promotion.

Why else would He tell us to "seek first the kingdom of God and his righteousness, and all these things will be added to you" (Matthew 6:33)? We aren't supposed to seek leadership for leadership's sake. It should be a consequence of others wanting to follow you. That's how Jesus operated. He never considered Himself a leader, as far as I can tell. He responded flatly to the disciples, "Truly, truly, I say to you, the Son can do nothing of his own accord, but only what he sees the Father doing" (John 5:19). He was only doing what He heard the Father tell Him to do. In other words, Jesus was a great follower. He laid aside His rights, His divinity, and His will to follow the Father.

Because Jesus is the Son of God, maybe making Him the linchpin of my argument feels unattainable. Fair enough. Let's look at Paul, then. If anyone was a leader, he was. He was instrumental in evangelizing much of the non-Jewish world. I'm gripped by what he said in his letters to the Corinthian church in 1 Corinthians 3 and 4. Paul was talking to the church about their obsession with leaders. Some were following Apollos, while others followed Paul. What does Paul say? "What then is Apollos? What is Paul? Servants through whom you believed" (1 Corinthians 3:5). He emphasized this again later in the same letter: "This is how one should regard us, as servants of Christ and stewards of the mysteries of God" (1 Corinthians 4:1). Okay, let's take a quiz, just to make sure we're all paying attention. How does Paul want us to regard him? As a leader or as a servant?

Still, we cling to our labels. We even invent terms like *servant leader*. We just can't bear to remove the word *leader* from our vernacular. Titles have replaced character, and we gladly sacrifice one for the other. We can't accept the fact that when a word comes to mean something else entirely, we'd be better off if we stopped using that word. Think of the many English words whose meanings have changed drastically over time. The word *dapper* originally meant "stout" or "heavyset" while *heartburn* described "lust or jealousy." *Inmate* was a term for any tenant, including residents of houses or dorms. *Bully* originally meant "superb or admirable," and *balderdash* was a strange mixture of liquids. In ancient Rome, a *matrix* was a term to describe a female animal kept for breeding.[2] You get my drift. I'd argue that since the word *leader* has come to mean a whole host of things that are incongruent with the gospel, we'd be better off not using it all. It's not in the Scriptures, anyway, so could the church go ahead and stop using the word *leader*? Just stop. Could we agree with Paul and simply be known as servants? Could we go back to names that carry a little less elitism? Shepherds were low-class citizens in Jesus's day. I'd think Paul would be confused by the "high-profile" pageantry leaders carry in the church today.

I recently heard a speaker at a fancy banquet say that Jesus actually coined the term *servant leader*. I recoiled. *No,* I thought, squirming in my seat, *Jesus didn't add the word* leader. *We did. Jesus just told us to be servants.* Why can't we tell people to serve and be done with it? Could it be that pastors in particular want so desperately to see their congregations rise up in service and acts of love that they lure them with a title? As Paul explains, "Christ's love compels us" (2 Corinthians 5:14, NIV). I would argue that by telling an egotistical person they'll be known as a "servant leader," we might be manipulating someone to serve who is compelled not by love but by a desire for accolades. Are we trying to tailor the way of Jesus to appeal to an unregenerate heart? I can't help but point out that it doesn't take a supernatural work of the Holy Spirit to want to be a leader, but it does take something extraordinary to delight in servanthood.

Jonathan Edwards used the term *common virtue* to describe

the human tendency to do good things out of pride or fear. In contrast, *true virtue* is doing the right thing because we trust God and want to obey Him.[3] We might say things such as, "You don't want to be forgotten, do you?" Or even, "You want to be a person of influence, right?" Don't you see it? Fear and pride are easy motivations to tap. That's when the label "leader" undermines the motivation to serve, because the promise is, "Hey, if you serve, you'll be a big deal." I don't think that's what Jesus was looking for. In fact, what comes to mind is a conversation with His disciples about who would be considered greatest in His kingdom. He told them, "Unless you change and become like little children, you will never enter the kingdom of heaven. Therefore, whoever takes the lowly position of this child is the greatest in the kingdom of heaven" (Matthew 18:3–4, NIV).

You might be thinking, *Okay, Mike, that's great and all, but it doesn't really help me. People are looking to me for a plan. Your theories about leadership don't change the fact that I'm the one in charge right now! I'm the head of a company, a family, a ministry. I have to lead or no one else will.*

Let me try to explain. When we realize that true leadership is a by-product of following well, we can exchange all those anxieties for something lighter. We can conserve all that frenetic energy we used to expend trying to live up to a label and be what everyone needed us to be. We can let go and focus on the voice of God. We can begin asking the right questions, such as: "What is Christ saying to me right now? How would He want me to treat my employees? How can I direct my energy toward building His kingdom and not my own? How can I serve the people who are looking to me for guidance?" Asking these questions is very different from trying to figure out how to leverage friendship and gain influence. Stop worrying about how much influence you have, and start concentrating on what to do with the influence you have right now.

My friend Brent Gambrell wrote a book on this topic called *Living for Another,* and I highly recommend it. Brent has an amazing ability to pack a whole lot of truth in a small package. His thoughts on submission hurt so good I took a picture of the pages. He argues, "Submission is the calling of every Christian." He cites Ephesians 5:21–23, which talks about mutual submission. He goes on, "Let's take the word *submit* back to its Greek origin. The word in Greek is *Hupotasso,* which means 'to arrange or assign under.' . . . To submit simply means that no matter the rank of the people in the room, I arrange myself at the bottom."[4] To clarify, Brent isn't saying you should mope around thinking about how insufficient you are. Rather, this is a call to focus on others so that your thoughts about yourself decrease.

Oh, wonderful! Everything is so much easier now! You might be scoffing to yourself as you read this. *Now I can just sit back, live my life, and think happy unicorn angel-face thoughts!* Of course, that's not how it works. It's been a painful process surrendering my credentials to God. It's constant work asking why I'm doing what I'm doing. It's constant work trying to consider others more than myself. It's constant work leaving the results up to God. But it's good work. It's soul work. I'm sure it will be no different for you. If we insist on letting grace name us, then our successes, our leadership, and our failures no longer define us.

Our accomplishments don't make us proud, and our mistakes no longer crush us. Grace keeps giving us a new name. It flips the importance of kingdoms upside down. It keeps us full of life even when some things need to die—namely, our obsession with ourselves.

The Naked Marine

The fundamental mistake is to begin with ourselves and not God. God is the center from
which all life develops. If we use our ego as the
center from which to plot the geometry of our
lives, we will live eccentrically.

—EUGENE H. PETERSON, *RUN WITH THE HORSES*

So how do we do it? How do we let go of our obsession with titles? How do we stop managing our reputations? I'm pretty sure it was the summer between my sophomore and junior year of college when I glimpsed how beautiful life could be when I stopped thinking about myself for more than two seconds. It happened during one of the scariest moments of my life, but the lesson was definitely worth the terror. My partner in crime, Jonny Rios (yes, the same guy who was driving when I was in the car accident) and I had come home from another long school year. He attended VMI. That's Virginia Military Institute for those who don't know. He was definitely in need of a break since VMI was a tough school. Some of the stories Jonny told me made me cringe. It sounded like higher education accompanied by a perpetual state of panic. I didn't know how he dealt with the pushups, the hazing, the middle-of-the-night workouts and marches, and all the other unmentionable insanity. I could never understand why he went there of his own free will. That summer break, I knew he needed to remember how to have fun. As it turned out, the fun almost killed us.

Jonny and I were driving on Interstate 95 one particularly muggy day when we noticed a large cliff towering above a body of water. It was right there off the interstate, just a mile north of exit 130 in Fredericksburg. Go check it out. It's still there. I remember pulling over and walking back up the side of the highway just to peer over the edge of the bridge. We wanted to be sure we weren't hallucinating. The two of us were experts at jumping from high things into water, so it didn't seem possible such a place existed in our hometown without our previous knowledge.

Mystified, we had to know how to get to this place. Smartphones weren't a thing yet, so we began driving in the direction we believed this wonderland to be. We drove around for about an hour until we finally pulled into a gated dirt road tucked behind a row of low-income housing. It was as if the gate was taunting us, tempting us to leave our car and continue on foot to discover our free-falling destiny. Problem was, on top of the gate rested a big old No Trespassing sign. We had a choice to make and we chose poorly. We ignored the sign and walked blissfully down the path until a vista opened before us. An old rock quarry, rimmed on one side by the cliffs we'd seen from the interstate, lay before us. It was now a dazzling crystal blue lake. We noticed a sign about scuba diving and deduced this was a private dive site of some sort. Without a word, we both stripped off our shirts and sprinted for the water.

We spent the whole day swimming, climbing, and cliff diving at our newfound private oasis. It was incredible. We envisioned spending the whole summer there with all our friends. Naturally, we couldn't keep the secret to ourselves, and the next day we brought the whole crew. There were seven of us who were "rolling deep," as the kids say. We parked both cars by the trailhead, again tramping past the No Trespassing signs and making our way to our secluded refuge. We were about to go for our fifth jump when the cop car drove out of the woods. It drove all the way out onto the beach across from us. From where we stood up on the cliff, we heard the loudspeaker boom across the lake: "Please come down off the rocks and make your way to the beach." One by one, we took one last plunge off the rocks and mournfully swam toward the flashing blue lights of infinite sadness.

When we broke the surface and scampered up on the shore, we saw a six-foot-five impossibly ripped marine leap out of a souped-up extended cab V12 Chevy Silverado. We hadn't seen the truck following the squad car while we were swimming, but standing there, wet and shivering, we knew this mountain of a man was undoubtedly a harbinger of doom. I didn't actually know if he was a marine, but he was wearing fatigues, his truck had a large *Semper Fi* sticker in the back window, and he looked like he wanted to eat me. His face was redder than a tomato, and his anger was like an electric current.

He thundered, "Do you boys have any idea what I could do to you for trespassing on my property?" We were frozen with fear. The sky began to turn black. Our hair stood on end. Our knees wobbled. "I will fine each of you five thousand dollars! You will spend at least six months in JAAIIII . . ."

He never finished the word. His tirade was cut short by some unknown force. His eyes crossed midsentence, and he let out a blood-curdling screech. "AAAGGGHHH." It sounded like brakes squealing. He began to tear at his clothes and rapidly tore off every stitch of clothing. He threw himself into the water, absolutely 100 percent naked. For the next five minutes, he flopped around like a beached dolphin, all the while screaming his murderous screams.

Now, I want you to picture the seven of us, staring with the intensity of a thousand suns, unable to begin to process what it was we were seeing. *Had this superhuman Avenger of a man completely lost his mind? Was he going to kill us? Was he demon possessed?* No.

He had pepper sprayed himself—in the crotch.

I'm not making this up. A full tank of liquid misery was loosed during his torrent of fury and had caused him to go into full-body convulsions. I guess if you get mad enough, and if you have a large bottle of pepper spray in your pants pocket, and if you're a hugely muscled man with an iron fist, you can actually squeeze hard enough to fire off the contents of that bottle into your shorts if you're not careful. He did. While he writhed in pain, none of us dared laugh, move, or breathe. We just stared on in perfect dread.

Eventually, after what must have been minutes but felt like hours, he gathered himself, swung a towel out of the bed of his truck, and wrapped it around his body. Without another look in our direction, he croaked, "Get. Out. Now." We grabbed our clothes and sprinted up the trail. A few moments later we collapsed in our cars, emotionally spent, amazed we had escaped alive. All at once, in a flood of hysteria, we burst into tears of laughter and relief. We drove away talking over one another. A few hours later, we were still shouting in disbelief, "Can you believe that happened?" It was incredible.

Even typing this story, I'm thinking, *There is no way anyone is going to believe this.* But it happened. And perhaps more incredibly, for a few moments, we had completely forgotten about ourselves. I realize it's an extreme example, but for those few moments of astonishment, while that poor marine flung himself back and forth, we didn't once think about ourselves. We were transfixed. We were free. I believe now that affirmation is not the cure for ego; wonder is. Nothing will cause you to forget about yourself like being caught up in awe of another.

Forget Finding Yourself

I hear a lot these days about finding oneself. Find your calling. Find your center. Find God's will for your life, perhaps. Maybe that's why you're reading this book in the first place. I'm all for introspection and self-understanding. I have some friends who point to the Enneagram as the key tool they used to save their marriage. But what I'm talking about here is adoration. The search for self-knowledge can quickly and subtly become a quest to adore ourselves. My humble opinion? I don't think we were meant to find our lives; we were meant to lose them. I'm pretty sure Jesus had a few things to say about that.[1]

In *I Am Not but I Know I Am,* Louie Giglio says it this way,

> We're invited to accept, as a free gift, rescue from sin's deadly flow and a place in God's eternal glory—a place we don't deserve, but one He offers to let us share in through the death of His Son. The one requirement is that we trade the starring role in the miserably small stories of us for supporting roles in the great Story of God.[2]

I love that. It's kind of like God is offering you and me a role equivalent to Samwise Gamgee in *The Lord of the Rings,* but we turn it down for the starring role in a local furniture-store commercial. Funny how that works. When we're not the center of attention, it can feel like a demotion—no matter the scale of the story we're being called into. It's a tough pill to swallow to realize my life isn't actually all about me. Talk about a death blow to pride. Eugene Peterson said, "We are not being led to see God in our stories but to see our stories in God's."[3]

It all comes back to understanding that our only focus is to follow. Yes, you are a follower, no matter how independent you feel. Though we don't like to admit it, we all follow something. We're all the sum of a vast number of things outside our own control and choices, such as gene pools, family trees, siblings, natural gifting, IQ, and childhood experiences. Our choices are important, but they're not the whole story. As Albert Camus said, "Life is the sum of all your choices." But if that's the whole equation, there's no room for mercy and grace.

I've heard it said we shouldn't be like thermometers and reflect the culture; we should be like thermostats in creating the culture. Sure, but here's the thing. While we definitely affect the environment around us, the environment affects us too. As much as we might want to be thermostats, we're also thermometers. We can obsess over this and even make our attempts to live for God's glory all about us, not Him. In our sinfulness, we can twist worthy goals such as being people of influence or leaving a legacy so that other people will see us and validate us.

As a member of a band that has had the opportunity to headline a show, I understand how absolutely delusional celebrity can make someone. As I said before, it's a really strange thing to be applauded for showing up to work. It's also strange to have meals catered for you, sound systems calibrated just for you, and drivers waiting to take you places, so that some days your biggest decision is what coffee shop you want to try. Everything revolves around the "star" of the show, right?

Well, as high and mighty as some shows can make you feel, a large summer festival can actually come as a welcome deflation of the ego. You might think that's crazy talk. Maybe you've been to a festival and you're thinking, "But festivals are even bigger than a normal show! That's got to be ten times worse!" Well, at a festival, no matter how big or famous your band is, there's a large group of people who are not there to see you play.

It seems like artists have been given a special ability to overlook the fans and see only the one or two people in the audience scowling with their arms crossed. It doesn't matter if there are five thousand people in the crowd having the time of their lives; you'd better believe we will not be able to stop looking at the two guys who look like their parents dragged them to the show as some sort of punishment. I remember playing before the rock group Skillet at a festival in Washington State. Right in the middle of an acoustic rendition of one of our songs, everyone in the front row started chanting "Skillet! Skillet! Skillet!" They were louder than I was, and I was singing through the sound system. Needless to say, I didn't walk off the stage that night thinking I was a big deal. However, I'm really thankful it happened. Turns out being booed and disregarded, while not great for my career, was much needed therapy for my soul.

The only thing that truly frees us from ourselves is God's love for us. Some people might say, "Oh, you're talking about narcissism. That's an easy fix. You need to quit thinking about yourself and love other people more!" Although I agree with that sentiment, often our motivations hold us back. You can't just get up and decide you're going to love people more. Try as you might, you can't change your own heart. Even if you do start loving people more as a result of your commitment, chances are you'll also begin to look down on anyone who doesn't love people as much as you do. On the other hand, if you fail to live up to your new resolution and you don't love others well, you'll most likely be drawn into self-condemnation for your lack of resolve. To quote the movie *Dan in Real Life,* "Love is not a feeling. . . . It's an ability."[4] I love that. In order to truly have the lasting ability to love another person selflessly and not as a means to feel better about ourselves, we must be fueled by the Father's heart. "We love because he first loved us" (1 John 4:19). If your obsession with yourself is growing while your love for others is fading, maybe you don't need to try to be more loving. Maybe you need to reacquaint yourself with the love God already has for you. You don't even need to try to think of yourself less; you only need to think about God's love more. His love crowds out our self-obsession.

God's love does not give us permission to think about how great we are. In fact, quite the opposite is true. The love of God frees us from ourselves. True freedom means not thinking too highly or too lowly of oneself. As Rick Warren wrote, "Humility is not thinking less of yourself; it is thinking of yourself less."[5] God loves us to free us. We talk a lot about God being for us, but sometimes we forget that the reason He is for us is so we can be for Him. He frees us from the crushing weight of narcissism so we can make much of Him. It's a paradox, but I've found it to be true. He frees us to follow the wisdom in the book of Proverbs: "Let another praise you, and not your own mouth" (27:2). What if I didn't have to tell everyone how great I am but was free to celebrate greatness in others? Besides, no one on this earth can make much of me often enough to fill me, but just a glimpse of God's glory fills me to overflowing.

The Disciple Jesus Loves

In John's first New Testament letter, he wrote, "In this is love, not that we have loved God but that he loved us and sent his Son to be the propitiation for our sins" (4:10). Whoa. Wait a second. Love isn't about what we do for God? Maybe you're a bit confused. Maybe you're still thinking God needs you to accomplish something really impressive for Him. Well, He doesn't. Jesus never asked us to change the world. He said to love one another.[6] I think this is an important and sobering distinction. The whole world doesn't have to be your concern. The people in your immediate vicinity do. Start loving and caring for the people around you and move outward. Your identity is not in how much change you can bring or in what you produce or accomplish. Let Jesus be enough of an accomplishment for you. Let your identity be the disciple Jesus loves.

Now, if you grew up in church you might respond, "The disciple Jesus loves? No, I'm not. John is. He was the disciple Jesus loved." Well, you're right and you're wrong. Let me explain. I also grew up in the church, and I can even remember the day my Sunday school teacher brought out the mighty flannelgraph board and began to teach us about the twelve disciples. Do you even know what a flannelgraph board is? If you don't know, Google it. It's paper presentation floating magic. Be amazed. My teacher used this powerful teaching tool as she began posting some cartoon cutouts to help us visualize ancient Israel.

"Here's Thomas, kids. He was a doubter. Oh, and here's Peter." Her smile turned disapproving. "He denied the Lord. And here is . . . ooh. Here's John." Her face began to glow. "John was Jesus's best friend. He was the disciple Jesus loved."

I remember my hand shooting up reflexively. "Oh! I want to be the disciple Jesus loves!"

She shook her head. "Mmm, sorry," she said. "John was.

I became hysterical. "But I want to be Jesus's best friend!"

"Sorry, dear . . . John."

I was devastated. Try as I might, I would never be one of Jesus's favorites. The job was already taken.

Or was it?

Several years later, I actually began to read the Bible for myself. Do you know what I found? The only place where John is referred to as "the disciple whom Jesus loved" is in the gospel he wrote.[7] Let that sink in. Can you imagine being one of the other disciples? I can imagine Peter reading the book to the others. "Well, here's the book John wrote. We're all in here. Thomas, Judas, John, the disciple Jesus loves . . . *Wait a minute!* The audacity! Everybody's gonna think he was the Lord's favorite! How dare he?"

This was either the most arrogant thing John could say or the most humble. I would argue it was the most humble. Here's why. Of all the disciples, John had the most room to brag. Since we love to let everyone know our accomplishments with every social media post we publish, it actually comes as a great shock when John doesn't call himself, "John, the disciple who laid his head on Jesus's chest." He also doesn't describe himself as, "John, the disciple who was given custody of Jesus's mother!" His public profile doesn't read, "I am John, the one disciple who stood at the cross while all the others flaked out and ran away." Instead of all those things, John referred to himself unthinkably as the disciple Jesus loved, which is such a beautiful example for us to follow. When you read John's other letters, this fits perfectly with his theology. This is why he wrote in 1 John 4 that it's all about God's love for us. Propitiation, by the way, is a big Bible word that can be translated simply this way: "We were going to get spanked, but Jesus put His butt in the way."

John had the most impressive resume of all the disciples, and yet, when identifying himself to the world, he didn't choose to mention what he could do or had ever done for God. Instead, he chose to brag about the love God had for him, not the love he had for God. This makes him shockingly different from many of us. We often seek to boost our self-esteem and let everyone know how great we are. We want to help others but make a point of announcing our good deeds online. It's no wonder Jesus told us not to let our left hands know what our right hands are doing.[8]

Growing up, I was told again and again, "Sin is missing the mark." But if that were the case, the Pharisees never sinned. Could we look deeper? Is there a fuller definition? What if sin is nothing more than an attempt to build an identity on something other than God and His love? Isn't that what we're after when we try to do things our way? Doesn't all sin begin with the simple lie "Maybe God doesn't love me?" Whether it's our shame and mistakes, or our success and achievements, we are all constantly being tempted in this way. We want to assert ourselves. We want to be remembered.

We think it's imperative for our obituary to boast about all the great things we did and the amazing impact we left. John's example offers us a better way. He wrote down his account of all that happened during Jesus's ministry, and then he described himself accurately. *Me? Who am I?* "Loved by Jesus. That's who I am." Amazing. No matter what happened or who would later drag his name through the mud, no matter his successes or failures, this identity could not be shaken. What about you? How will you be remembered? What about me? How do we want the world to see us? Do we need others to see what we've done, or is it enough to point them to what has been done for us? It might sound silly, but put this book down for a minute and go find a mirror. Look yourself in the eyes, and with all the humility you can muster, repeat John's simple soul-saving words, "I am the disciple Jesus loves."

Mountains Not Mirrors

A weird thing happened when I was told Jesus would take my burdens. People ask me all the time about my conversion story, so I've broken it into three phases. I was six years old when I learned Jesus would take my guilt and my shame and all the judgment for all the dumb things I ever did. I said, "Wait . . . Jesus will take my spanking for me? Sign me up!" *Boom.* I prayed the prayer and Jesus became my Savior. But Lord? He didn't become my Lord until the end of high school when I started letting Him disagree with me. I think that's the basis of any true relationship, isn't it? To have a friendship with anyone, they must reserve the right to have a different opinion. Otherwise, we're just in a relationship with ourselves. God is no different. So He was my Savior at six but not my Lord until eighteen. And Jesus didn't become my treasure until I got to college and began to have a sense of His sweetness in my soul.

Savior.

Lord.

Treasure.

It seems to me that a lot of us get a handle on the first two but then slide through life trying to please a God who isn't really pleasing to us. If you never grow to treasure Christ in your soul, the whole call to obedience will feel like a heavy chain instead of freedom. As we get older, something suspicious happens. If we aren't careful, the burden of our shame is replaced with a different but equally heavy burden. We're told we were saved so that we can go save others. Our guilt is on the Savior's shoulders, but now the task of saving the world is on ours. We'd better come through.

Yet, Jesus said He'd replace our heavy burden with one that is light.[9] I think the reason we trade one burden for another is that we still haven't been released from our self-fixation. I like what my friend Phillip's grandfather quipped the other day, "It's not your job to change the world. Jesus already did that."

Social media tries to convince me otherwise. As a singer in a band, I have a love/hate relationship with social media on every level. I love connecting with people who've had radical experiences with our songs. I also love showing people we're just normal, ridiculous, silly dudes, hacking our way through life like everyone else. I love engaging questions and raising awareness for social issues and other important topics. But on the flip side, social platforms make me tired. Facebook, Instagram, Twitter, the list goes on. Around every corner, promoters, label execs, and fans are all evaluating the art you make by the number of followers you have. So it quickly becomes a numbers game. The internet can change from being a place to learn and care for others to a brand-building mechanism. Suddenly, we're no longer just building an online scrapbook of sorts; instead, we're publishing snapshots of the product we want to sell. And the product is ourselves.

Increasingly, I'm seeing posts from friends, saying, "Taking a week to refocus." "Need a break. Be back in a week." Do you have friends saying similar things? Even small posts like these testify to the fact that being so focused on ourselves isn't working. I can't help but chuckle to myself when I think of how evident it is. "Did you really need to tell us you're going off your socials? Why not . . . you know . . . just go off them?" I can't help but stop and think, *What on earth are we using the internet for?* We thought it would connect us, but the comparison seems to be driving us further apart.

I wrestle with how much to post. I do. If I don't find it healthy to be constantly looking at my phone, should I be creating content that keeps other people glued to theirs? I know, I know. You can say the same thing for movies or even books, for that matter. Admittedly, I may be tempted in ways others aren't. I often come back to social streams, hoping someone is talking about me. Again, I'm probably the only one who does this, right?

Joe's Basecamp, a local gym in Sydney, Australia, boasts the motto: "Mountains not mirrors." I resonate with that thought. I've never once pulled my head up from an hour-long social media compliment-craving binge fest and thought, *Ah. I feel so enlightened. All those people talking about me has really elevated my being to a new level of consciousness. This time, I am satisfied.* That's hyperbole, but you get my drift. We never get free by thinking about ourselves; freedom comes from forgetting ourselves.

Whether we climb to the top of a mountain, gaze into the eyes of our beloved, or care for the poor in their distress, we experience the wonder of self-forgetfulness. In his treatise, *The Freedom of Self-Forgetfulness,* Timothy Keller vamps on C. S. Lewis for a moment. He writes:

> C.S. Lewis in *Mere Christianity* makes a brilliant observation about gospel-humility at the very end of his chapter on pride. If we were to meet a truly humble person, Lewis says, we would never come away from meeting them thinking they were humble. They would not be always telling us they were a nobody (because a person who keeps saying they are a nobody is actually a self-obsessed person). The thing we would remember from meeting a truly gospel-humble person is how much they seemed to be totally interested in us. Because the essence of gospel-humility is not thinking more of myself or thinking less of myself, it is thinking of myself less.
>
> Gospel-humility is not needing to think about myself. Not needing to connect things with myself. It is an end to thoughts such as, 'I'm in this room with these people, does that make me look good? Do I want to be here?' True gospel-humility means I stop connecting every experience, every conversation, with myself. In fact, I stop thinking

about myself. The freedom of self-forgetfulness. The blessed rest that only self-forgetfulness brings.[10]

This is especially difficult in today's modern age, when promoting yourself on social media has become such a large part of our everyday lives. It's even required for most jobs now. We're all clamoring for more power and influence, and to accomplish that we have to engage with our followers. But what if God doesn't need us to protect our power? I've been in situations when I knew speaking the truth on a social media platform would cause me to lose followers. In those moments, I've taken great comfort in the truth that Jesus doesn't need me to preserve my reputation, my legacy, or my precious influence. Fact is, my job as His disciple isn't to be popular; it's to tell the truth. When I take my eyes off myself, the freedom to live in love instead of chasing "likes" is breathtakingly clear. So, whether it takes an Instagram fast, a harrowing encounter with a naked Marine, or gazing at a mountain range, I pray God reveals His love to your spirit in such a profound way that it frees you, for a few glorious moments, to forget yourself.

9

God Doesn't Need You

> "The beautiful is as useful as the useful." He added, after a moment's silence, "Perhaps more so."
>
> —Victor Hugo, *Les Misérables*

In January of 2016, our entire band along with our wives gathered in our drummer's living room. We had called an emergency meeting at Jason's house because we had just finished one of the busiest touring years we had ever had. We had reached a breaking point due to the stressful schedule and our general lack of monetary success. There was an awkward heaviness in the room. Many of us were wondering if this was the beginning of the end of the band. My wife, Kelly, said she couldn't take it anymore. She felt like she was raising our kids by herself and like she was married to a stranger. She was in tears, looking around the room to see if she was the only one who felt that way. She wasn't. I sat there, breathless, beholding the scene, wondering if my family was going to be yet another casualty on the altar of ministry and ambition.

Something my mentor had said rang in my ears: "Remember, Mike, God's not served by men's hands as if He needed anything." All those years I worked at a church came rushing back. Andrew Oates was my boss and oversaw all the student and college ministries. We spent a lot of time together, and one of the things he talked about frequently was the danger of burning out from ministry. He repeated Acts 17:24–25 almost every day: "The God who made the world and everything in it, being Lord of heaven and earth, does not live in temples made by man, nor is he served by human hands, as though he needed anything, since he himself gives to all mankind life and breath and everything." He had been in ministry for quite a while before we met, so he wanted to save me from wrong thinking. Over the years, I began to see why he was warning me.

Too many well-meaning "laborers in the Lord" couldn't say no to opportunity. They couldn't understand that ministry effectiveness and outcomes weren't resting on their shoulders, though it might have felt that way. So many people I worked with sacrificed their families on the altar of ministry, and as a result, their families fell apart. There were affairs and breakdowns. Some had to quit ministry altogether. The list of issues goes on. I didn't want any of that to happen to my family and me. As hard as it was to consider, in that moment in Jason's living room, I was ready to call it quits. Our band might have to dissolve, but I wasn't going to destroy my family in the name of God.

After more than a few hours of awkward conversation and asking tough questions, we decided on a plan B, which we called an evacuation plan. We all agreed we'd give it one more year, if we could agree on a reasonable number of shows that would allow our home lives to remain healthy. Instead of doing another 140 shows, as we'd just done that year, we decided to try to keep the number around 90. We didn't know if we'd be able to live on that, but we figured it was worth a shot. If God didn't provide, then we would all look for something else to do. Maybe I could finally go into Navy SEAL training. God didn't need us, after all, so we took the plunge.

We committed to doing fewer shows, and for the next twelve months, God tested our resolve. That's how it always goes. Calls came in offering more and bigger shows, but we kept our hard line of 90 shows. We stuck to it. Other strange things started happening. Our stage manager was offered a better job he couldn't turn down. Our merchandise manager was asked to personally assist a big country star. Our lighting guy got a job running lights for a much busier artist, and our sound man got a job offer from some random worship singer named Chris Tomlin. Our overhead shrank significantly, and it was all largely beyond our control.

A year later, we had our annual Christmas party. It was the first time we and all our wives were together again, this time at our guitarist's house. In Jeff's living room, the atmosphere couldn't have been more different. Instead of shifting glances, there were embraces. Instead of a storm of questions, there was renewed vision for the future of our band. Not only had we met all the financial goals we had put into place, but we'd done it by performing 50 fewer shows. Most importantly, our hearts felt full, and our families were connected and thriving.

Let me pause here, because there's going to be a teenager who reads that and says, "See, Dad! I should be able to do half as many chores and get paid the same! Jesus is awesome!" That's not what I'm saying. I include this story to illustrate that if God calls you to something, He doesn't want you to sacrifice your emotional, spiritual, or physical health in order to accomplish it. If He calls you to a thing, He will also provide you the grace to do it. Sometimes the thing you're asked to give up is something you can't get back. We had been so concerned with how successful we needed to be to provide for our families that we almost lost them. We learned that God didn't need us to be successful. He wanted us to be surrendered. It didn't matter to Him how many shows we played or how many number-one songs we released. What mattered to Him was how we went about playing shows and getting our songs on the chart. What mattered most was whether we would give Him our dreams.

Why is that so important? I've witnessed in my own life that when my relationships start crumbling because I'm so dead set on my dream and the way it should go, that dream usually isn't God's calling for me. Instead, it's really just my idol. If God calls, He will provide. He will equip. The outcome may look different from what I had planned. But by handing over the future of our careers, we went from wondering if God could provide to experiencing His abundant provision firsthand.

I hope you experience this truth for yourself. Maybe you've

been stuck in a career or some other pursuit you felt you couldn't turn down. Maybe you've wrapped your hands so tightly around your life that you can't even receive from God. It's okay. You can let go. You'll be amazed at what God will do when you realize He doesn't need you. Instead, He just wants you.

What if I told you that your loveliness to God doesn't rise and fall with your usefulness? Do you think you could receive that? Do you think you could possibly believe God can go on saving the world without you? Can you live in such a way that makes you more or less useful to God? Sure. But in Christ you aren't—and will never be—any less lovely to Him, no matter how much you're doing for Him. He can really get along fine without your help, but He'll never stop wanting your heart. Let that statement cover you like a warm blanket. He doesn't love you because He needs you. He doesn't love you because you're useful. You are not a commodity to Him. You are His treasure, which He gave everything to win back. He doesn't need you. He wants you. Ironically, accepting a love like that will make you useful. In my ministry experience, I've been most effective when I didn't need to be involved in ministry to convince myself I had worth.

Doing Less, Loving More

When I started working in a college ministry my junior year of college, I met a guy named Cory. Cory and I are still friends. He is loyal, feisty, and downright hilarious. Cory is one of a kind. Cory almost drowned in a pool when he was three years old. He experienced brain damage from the lack of oxygen and as a result, his speech is jerky and oftentimes tediously slow. He also has impaired motor skills. His mind is sharp, but sadly, his body can't keep up. Though he has a wicked sense of humor, most people are too impatient trying to talk with him that they never get to experience it.

When I first met Cory, I had trouble slowing down and taking the time to listen. But as I observed others interacting with him, I realized how petty I was being. I vividly remember one Sunday morning. I had just finished another college group service at the church, and much to my chagrin, I once again witnessed students talking to Cory for a short time until they inevitably started feeling awkward. They began looking over his shoulder for ways to escape the conversation. I understand how hard it can be to talk with someone who speaks four or five times slower than you do. Most people would start shuffling their feet and look quickly around the room while Cory went on talking in his slow and cumbersome way, and then they would say, "Uh huh. Well . . . uh . . . I have to go. See you next week, Cory!"

These moments crushed my heart, because Cory and I had become friends. I knew it took him a while to articulate his thoughts, but Cory was funny and caring. Some of the times I've laughed the hardest were with Cory. Though it took patience, he was a good friend to me. Sadly, I watched many of my classmates—perhaps too concerned with efficiency and effectiveness—pass right over Cory because they just didn't have the time to give him. Sometimes, doing less means loving more. Accomplishing less with our time can often mean loving the people around us more meaningfully. Surprisingly, learning to recognize Cory's value freed me from my own anxieties. I began to realize that God didn't need my production as much as He wanted my presence.

Last week in church, I had a similar feeling. A baby was crying in the back, and it was as if the air was being sucked out of the room. The sanctuary seemed transformed into an airplane cabin. The poor mom was trying to soothe her infant's needs, while everyone around her quietly obliterated her with stares of white-hot fury. As a father, I'm particularly sensitive to moments like these. I wanted to stand up and declare, "We were all babies once! Let's give this woman some empathy! Interruption is a part of life. It's going to be okay!"

I wished the pastor would stop the service and address the tension. I wanted him to say, "In the kingdom of God, unlike air travel, we are willing to inconvenience ourselves for this dear mother. We don't even have to finish this sermon, if we need to remind this mom she is deeply loved, even if her baby's cries are inconvenient. What if we all embraced the interruption this morning so we can love her more?" Imagine that. Seems to me that it's not much use learning more if we aren't loving the people right in front of us more. In the world, the few must sacrifice their needs for the many, but the gospel flips this on its head. The many and powerful instead sacrifice themselves for the few and the weak. Look no further than Jesus as proof. He says the Father leaves the ninety-nine to save one. He Himself is worthy of all praise and yet strips off His divinity to save sinners.

Let's take a step back here for a second and remind ourselves that for the King of the universe to spend time with any of us is, in fact, a gigantic waste of His time. It is essentially a disadvantage for Jesus to move toward us. Think about it. Any step toward us is a step toward someone more insignificant. For God to send His beloved Son to earth is a move of the superior toward the inferior. Therefore, we can rest assured He moves toward us because He wants us, not because He needs us.

You might be thinking, *What? This guy doesn't know the Bible at all. Of course, God needs me! I'm His hands and feet! I'm His ambassador! I'm His voice to the world!* Yes, we are His hands and feet. Paul even adds in his second letter to the Corinthians: "We are therefore Christ's ambassadors, as though God were making his appeal through us. We implore you on Christ's behalf: Be reconciled to God" (5:20, NIV). However, just because God wants to use us, does that mean He needs to use us? Absolutely not. Don't forget what Paul said earlier in the same letter: "We have this treasure in jars of clay to show that this all-surpassing power is from God and not from us" (4:7, NIV). Paul essentially calls us brittle mud pots. In Paul's time, household vessels were homely, unimpressive, and easily broken. Why would Paul describe us this way? He goes on to explain that the power to transform lives isn't from us but from God! He uses us, broken as we are, still learning, still struggling, still falling forward, so people will know that real and lasting change comes from Him.

Here's my warning if we won't accept this. If we don't believe what we read in Acts 17, that God really doesn't need us, then we could completely miss the gift of joy that was meant to motivate our obedience in the first place. We could even be serving God in a way that blasphemes Him. If we serve God because we think He can't get along without us, then we act as if He is less than all-powerful. As my dad used to say to me, "I brought you into this world, and I can take you out of it." God has every right to say the same to us.

Consider the Sabbath. I've heard many scholars speculate that the reason God established the Sabbath was to remind humanity that He doesn't love us because of our productivity. I couldn't agree more. When you live in a culture that idolizes the ability to make a profit and equates it to virtuous living, it can be nearly impossible to take a day off. When we're out there "killing it," we feel more worthy. Making money isn't wrong, of course, but it also isn't necessarily right. We ought to concern ourselves with our motivations for and methods of making money. Jesus isn't nearly as concerned with maximizing our potential as He is with purifying our potential. Believe me, it's not the same thing. The Sabbath is a chance to remember that the world will go on without you.

10

I Stopped Asking God to Use Me

It is amazing what you can accomplish
if you do not care who gets the credit.

—HARRY S. TRUMAN

'll never forget the day I stopped asking God to use me. I did. I
quit cold turkey. It was about eight years ago, and I was in Wisconsin for Lifest, one of the first summer festivals our band ever
played. We were backstage, huddled in our van trying to escape
the early afternoon sun, praying before our set. I was cheating and
my eyes were open a little, as I watched the other more notable
artists going back and forth from their buses to the catering tent.
I found it hard to concentrate as I wondered what it would be like
to be at their level. What would it be like to have a ministry like
theirs? Imagine influence like that! I tried to pray harder. I shut my

eyes and doubled down, "Use us, God! Oh Father, use our set immensely for Your glory!" Of course, God saw right through my noble pleas. I could almost feel a physical tap on my shoulder as I heard the Spirit whisper, *But what if I want to use the other bands?* Ouch. That hurt. I knew exactly where this was going. God was showing me the prayer behind my prayer.

Has that ever happened to you? Even though I was ostensibly asking Him to use my band, what I was really asking was for Him to use me more than the other bands. It wasn't a prayer of offering myself to His service. It was a prayer of asking that my service ascribe worth to me. I might have been saying, "Use us for Your glory!" But what I really meant was "Use us for our glory." It was a subtle but subversive distinction.

When I first started playing music with my band, I believe my most of my motives were pure. For years, we prayed the same prayer before every show: "God, please use our band. What could be better than doing what we love in a way that's useful to You?" We wanted to be a light to the world and help set the captives free. Over time, though, my heart subconsciously shifted. Even though I was still praying the same words, "God, use our band," in my heart I was really praying, "God, use our band more than the other bands." As crazy as it sounds, it was no longer enough to be used by God. I needed to be used more than everyone else. Ironically, I've often found that to be true in many areas of my life. It's usually my good works that keep me from clinging to Christ, not my bad ones.

That hot July day, God quietly challenged my prayers, helping me see how comparison had dug its ugly claws into me. He simply suggested, *What if I want to use the other bands?* But this question was enough to cause me to change course. God gave me an entirely new prayer to pray, and I've never prayed the same way since. Now, instead of asking to be used, I simply ask God to move. I no longer pray, "God use me." I pray, "God use anyone." Whether He uses me, my band, a volunteer, or another artist, it doesn't change my potential for joy. With this prayer, I'm celebrating how God is moving, whether I'm in the picture or not. I find that the more I celebrate others, the more joyful I become. Let me say it this way: Celebration keeps me from comparison and jealousy. When I focus my energies on lauding others and not on outdoing them, ten times out of ten I get more joy, not less.

Oftentimes, though, we do the opposite. Instead of passing out high fives of congratulations, we talk smack about those doing better than us. We think we need to hold back our compliments to protect our little slice of glory, as if there's not enough to go around. All the while, we could be getting an extra helping. These are the supernatural mathematics of celebration. The more we celebrate others, the more joy there is. We're not fighting over the same piece of pie. God is even offering us an extra share of joy if we would willingly offer up our share of the applause. The victories of others become ours. Your victories become mine. How beautiful it is that our sorrow lessens when divided among friends and our joy multiplies?

I had this conversation with my friend Gareth the other day. Gareth is one of the founding members of an Irish worship band called Rend Collective. We both agreed we had been stifling our own joy, trying to be used more than everyone else. After our talk, he turned around and wrote a song called "Counting Every Blessing." It might be my favorite of the songs he's written too. The more we count our blessings, it would seem, the more there are to share.

The Day My Dove Award Died

Have you heard of the Dove Awards? It's an award show for "Christian" music. I use quotation marks because music can't personally decide to follow Jesus, can it? Can a song be a Christian? Or is it a song written by a Christian? I know what people mean, though. Christian music is the genre label people use to define a particular group of songs by their content. It's strange for sure. Apart from instrumental music, it's the only genre defined by using an adjective. There are some tricky ramifications, such as when hip-hop, hard rock, and folk artists are lumped into the "Christian" category because their songs have religious themes. No other genre does that. While slapping the word *Christian* onto music can be confusing, using it as an adjective can be dangerous. What if a "Christian" song isn't actually any good? Are we associating Jesus with bad music then? What if a "Christian" artist is ripping off another song? Is it still plagiarism? Worse, what if a "Christian" song says something that doesn't line up with Scripture? John Newton wrote the song "Amazing Grace" to the tune of a popular bar song. Does that mean it's not really "Christian?" I think we do better keeping the word *Christian* as a noun rather than an adjective. I know I, for one, would much rather be called a Christian for the way I live than for the music I make. Would it be overly complicated to call me a Christian who makes music, instead of a Christian musician? I suppose it's too much of a mouthful to call the genre "songs that talk about Jesus," but it would definitely be more accurate.

But I digress. What was I talking about? Oh, yes. The Dove Awards. Now, don't get me wrong. It may sound like I'm bashing my genre. I'm not. I love songs about Jesus, and I've learned to love the Dove Awards. God has taught me so much through the discipline of celebrating others.

Some have referred to the Dove Awards as the Jesus Grammys. I've heard stories of artists both praising and condemning nights like it. Personally—and I haven't always thought this way, mind you—I think a night of celebrating one another is a wonderful discipline for artists who get up and talk about themselves every day. Award shows can be beautiful if our hearts are looking to give affirmation. They can go quite wrong as well—if we're bent solely on garnering attention for ourselves. Comparison, when it only validates our egos, has no place in God's kingdom. When we do find jealousy and comparison lurking in our hearts, we do well to celebrate our way out of it as quickly as we can.

Our band has won a couple of awards, but God quickly made His point about comparison when our song "By Your Side" won Song of the Year in 2010. I honestly was overjoyed when our name was announced. I felt amazing as I held the award and delivered what was obviously a very humble and gripping acceptance speech. I thought, *I've got to be the most humble winner this stage has ever seen.* There was no way I was letting that little statue dictate my worth before my peers. Until . . . the bottom fell out. More accurately, the bottom of the award fell off. Right after I delivered my glowing address, the trophy girl escorted me backstage, and the bottom part of our Dove award clattered to the floor. Our prestigious award straight up self-destructed. I guess the glue gun wasn't working that day. The stage manager whipped around and shot me a glare that said "Get out of my backstage or be destroyed." I stood there looking at my deconstructed bronze bird, realizing it reflected my deconstructed pride. I had to laugh.

I gathered up the pieces of my pride and our award and scurried around the corner. A college-age volunteer with a headset was standing in the corridor. She grabbed my arm as I passed by. "Hey," she said. "You don't know me, but I wanted to tell you about that song you just won that award for . . ." She broke off, looking confusedly at the remains of the trophy balanced in my arms. She regrouped. "That song"—tears welled up instantly— "my roommate played that song for me last year, and it was the first time I believed in the love of God."

I think I just stared at her with my mouth open. Unlike my perfectly crafted speech, I was now at a loss for words. I wanted to chuck the maimed Dove down the hall. I was already being rushed to a press room by more people with headsets, but I managed to form some thoughts at last. "Thank you, thank you, thank you. That is why we do this! Not for these awards. Your story is the award." I was halfway yelling to her by the time I turned the corner. I didn't even get her name, but she gave me the greatest gift I could have received that night. When all the complicated jeans, sequined tops, and bright lights blur your vision, one sentence was all it took to clarify mine. I'm not here on the earth to win awards. I am here to believe my heart is God's reward. So is yours.

I have this audacious belief now. God isn't up in heaven wringing His hands, wondering how He's going to save the world without us. He doesn't need us to acquire fame or notoriety or leverage our influence for maximum impact. He may even need us to stop trying to expand our territory, so He can expand His kingdom in the territory of our hearts. He owns the whole deal, anyway. He owns all the cattle on all the hills,[1] so He isn't fretting the way we are. He's got us covered. He's got our backs. Even after coming to earth to save the world, Jesus worked in anonymity well into adulthood before performing any miracles at all. I forget that. The son of God was chilling as a carpenter from the historically Podunk town of Nazareth for almost three decades. God in the flesh was carving chairs. If that doesn't reorient your self-importance, I don't know what will. If He came today, Jesus would have been helping you assemble your Ikea furniture. If that's not beneath Him, then maybe we can quit clinging to our reputations and seeking adulation. We already have God's vote. He's handing out awards that never fall apart in our hands. His awards have better titles too. Instead of "Song of the Year," His awards say "Daughter," "Son," "Friend." These are names we share. When we share them, there's no risk of losing ours. Artists of the Year will come and go, but being His child is the one award we can never lose.

Now What?

So why serve at all, then? If God doesn't need me or the things I do or the songs I write, why do anything at all? Why even get out of bed in the morning? I'm God's treasure no matter what I do, so now what? Well, since God didn't create you and me because He was lacking something, He must ask us to serve as a way to live out our innate gifts and passions. I have to believe His urging us to serve and to love is because participation with Him is how life works best. Life is a celebration, not a competition. God wired us to commune with Him in everything we do. Serving Him is an opportunity to turn every breath into a big, fat thank-you. We love God back. We serve Him back. He initiates and we can't help but respond. We participate because we've been welcomed into His work. It's not that He can't do it without me; it's that He knows I can't do it without Him.

God longs for relationship with us, not our productivity or accomplishments. Although, we can go too far and assume He made us because He was lonely. I'm quite convinced loneliness was not the reason God created humans. I believe in the mysterious doctrine of the Trinity and that the Father made us from the overflow of the joy He had in communing with the Son and Holy Spirit. Since He made us in His image, that perfect relationship shapes us. We were made by Him and for Him, by community and for community, by relationship and for relationship. That, I believe, is why God created the world, and it's what He created us to do. It's as if God were saying, "This thing we got? This other-centered, other-honoring, other-celebrating, always-sharing relationship of perfect union? We can't contain it. We have to let someone else in on it. We have to create some people so they can get in on this."

This is why God isn't selfish when He asks us to glorify Him.

He is actually asking to do what He's already been doing for eternity. The Father glorifies the Son. The Spirit glorifies the Son. The Son glorifies the Father.[2] This blows my mind. When God tells us to glorify Him, we are only being asked to do what God did first. Celebrating, honoring, serving, loving . . . we are called to do what He did first. Then everything changes. Work comes from a place of rest. We stop living for God and experience the sweetness of living because of God. We don't snatch away celebration from others; we pass it on as if we had more than we know what to do with. Our loveliness to God doesn't rise and fall with our usefulness. We're His kids, His friends, and His beloved. We're not a resource; He delights in us and lavishes His grace on us. We'll never pay it back, so breathe a big sigh of relief. We get to turn around and do the same for others. Competition has lost its power over us. Nobody is a threat. Instead, they are a reflection of the Trinity. They are relationship. They are shared space. One body, yet we are all different parts. We can throw out the old broken awards of recognition, and we can even stop keeping tabs on who is the best. Yes, we might be amazed at how wasteful our lives start to seem, but we'll also find that's when grace works best.

11

Wasting Time on God

Pray continually . . . this is God's will for you.
—1 Thessalonians 5:17–18 (niv)

I was always terrible at praying. For years, no matter how hard I tried, I just couldn't do it. I'd lock myself in my closet, but instead of savoring God's goodness, I would end up reorganizing. I tried waking up with the sun. I would jump out of bed and kneel down on my bedroom floor. Thirty minutes later, I would wake up in a puddle of my own drool. I recited the Lord's Prayer. I memorized the ACTS prayer acrostic.[1] I tried. I really did. None of my prayer strategies worked. I was ready to give up on the idea that I would ever be able to establish anything resembling a consistent prayer life, when all of a sudden, it happened. It was an otherwise ordinary day when I finally learned how to pray.

I was two years out of college at the time, still working as an intern at the church in South Florida, and once more I had risen at dawn only to fall back asleep at the foot of my bed. Shaking myself free from slumber and spittle, I grabbed my Bible in frustration and walked out the door to the field behind the house I was living in. Marching resolutely around the field, I was committed to staying awake. That was really it. I wasn't trying to commune with God as much I was just trying not to fall back asleep.

It worked.

I marched and ranted up to the heavens. In my twenty-odd years of life, I had prayed aloud in public settings and worship events, but I had never done that in my personal prayer time. Something changed. I was still holding my Bible loosely in one hand, swinging it along beside me as I began to talk about my inability to stay awake. "God! What's wrong with me? Why can't I stay awake? Am I a fake Christian? Is this whole thing with You pretend or what?"

I'd shout a couple of questions and then read a few verses. All the while, I just kept marching. I felt foolish mumbling to myself. I was self-conscious, wondering if someone was watching. To anyone peering over the gate and into the field, I must have looked like a sweaty-toothed madman running into a spider web, grasping at the air and flailing about. It didn't matter. I had to find my way. I didn't care what I looked like if it meant I might actually achieve some sort of communion with the Lord. It was a foolishness I was ready to take on.

Outside, out loud, and moving, I prayed. I didn't care who was watching or who was misunderstanding. If Jesus was totally fine with being misunderstood, I could be fine with it too. That muggy day in Florida, I found my spiritual footing by simply keeping my feet moving. I was storming around in the grass, muttering aloud, but I managed to pray for more than five minutes. It was exhilarating.

I don't know what it will take for you, but for me these three simple steps have helped my easily distracted brain stay on course:

- Go outside.
- Pray out loud.
- Keep moving.

It is essential for each of us to find some method by which we can return our minds to communion with God, because perpetual communion is what our God is after.

Keep Asking; Keep Resting

I have to admit, I find 1 Thessalonians 5:17–18 both frustrating and humorous: "Pray continually, give thanks in all circumstances; for this is God's will for you in Christ Jesus" (NIV). Essentially, Paul was saying that God's will for your life is to keep praying. It's almost as if Paul said "Hey, you want to figure out God's will for your life? Okay. Keep asking Him what it is." Thanks so much, Paul. While this seems impossible or even like it might be a joke, I think God is always trying to bend our will to His. What better way than to ask us never to stop conversing with Him? But often we don't like that, because we don't want to keep asking. We don't want to keep moving. We want to live life on cruise control. We want our course mapped out, the speed set, and our feet kicked up on the dash.

Maybe it's just me, but I think I'd rather have God just tell me what to do, and then I can go do it. I want to plug the destination into my phone and let the GPS do the work. But instead, it seems that God wants to sit next to me while keeping all the directions to Himself. He wants me waiting on His every word. "Oh, oh! Turn right here!" But who wants to live like that? I don't want to keep checking gauges and speed. I don't want to keep driving if I don't know where I'm going. I don't want to have to keep listening! I'd rather God just have a big heavenly chalkboard somewhere, with every step listed in perfect detail. It would be so much easier to chart my progress. "Okay, God, what do you want me to do? Oh, okay. Got it. Next? Help an old lady? Check. Give to the poor? Check. Give me a task and I'll get it done." But that's not what this verse is saying. It's saying, "Whatever you're doing, wherever you're going, be with God."

I think that's why for most of us prayer feels like an epic waste of time. It feels like an unnecessary stop on the road trip because someone has to pee. Don't believe me? Go pray for twenty minutes right now. I'm not kidding. Put the book down. Go somewhere quiet, and just sit there. Or if you're like me, walk around outside. Chances are you can't. You've got bigger fish to fry. You have to get things done, right? It's only natural to think that way. That's how the world works, isn't it? We'll be fired if we're inefficient at our jobs, so why would God be any different? Perform, perform, perform. Isn't that what the Almighty is asking of us?

Last year, my wife and I were gifted a short week's vacation by a close friend, to sit and do nothing by the ocean. We jumped at the opportunity. I was coming off a crazy year of touring, and my sweet wife—mother to our then three, now four, young children—

was ready for a break. The trip was rejuvenating. We basically sat in a pool and looked at the ocean all day, every day. But nothing was better than hearing the voice of my Father. After a couple of days of unwinding and letting my performance-hungry ego starve through inactivity, the morning of our third day I woke with the sunrise. I sat watching the waves and sipped the overly complicated cup of coffee I had made with my travel grinder and scale. (Don't knock it until you've tried it.) I let out a long, slow exhale. *Breathe,* I said to myself. *Take it all in.* Suddenly, three words began running through my heart and my head: *Work from rest.* Over and over. It didn't stop. I shook my head and looked at the sky. It was inescapable. *Work from rest. Work from rest. Work from rest.* This phrase didn't stop running through my mind all day.

I don't know how you hear the voice of God or even if you believe it's possible. But for me, when a word, phrase, or idea that aligns with Scripture grabs hold of my subconscious and won't let go, I can't help but feel it's from Him. In this instance, I began thinking of Jesus's words in Matthew: "Come to me, all who labor and are heavy laden, and I will give you rest. Take my yoke upon you . . . [It] is easy, and my burden is light" (11:28–30).

Easy and light. Does that describe your prayer life? Shoot. Does it describe any aspect of your life? Is it a prevalent characteristic of the "leaders" you look up to? Does ease and lightness mark the lives of your spiritual fathers and mothers? The cultural ethos we've had burned into our brains since we were kids has been "Work hard, play hard." Work as hard as you can, and then you get your much-deserved rest. "Work *for* rest." That's what we're told to do. Most of us don't even suspect there could be another way. Is working *from* rest an idea for the lazy? Is it just an impractical fantasy?

These are tough questions that don't always have simple answers. However, I'm learning more and more that God doesn't want me to be in chaos. He wants me to rest. He wants me to have a deep unshakable joy in my soul. He wants me to really act like I'm accepted. If He makes me a leader, it's not so I can gain everyone's approval; it's so I can share this principle with them. Dreaming that depends on surrender. Serving that involves receiving. This is the way of rest Jesus came to show us. All is surrender. All is His. Follow Him, and He will make you fishers of men.

The Right Fight

Dallas Willard once said, "Grace is opposed to earning, not to effort."[2] I think that's a distinction worth noting.

It makes sense, though. If God is indeed a God of grace, it makes sense that He wouldn't ask us to pray as a way of talking Him into action. He said to King Solomon, "If my people who are called by my name humble themselves, and pray and seek my face and turn from their wicked ways, then I will hear from heaven and will forgive their sin and heal their land" (2 Chronicles 7:14). Humble yourselves, pray, and seek God's face. Seeking God's face is not the same thing as seeking His hand. He wasn't saying, "If my people would just put enough time in, then I'll give 'em five golden prayer stars, and once the chart is full, I'll give them a prize!" Of course not. His admonition to pray without ceasing must be an invitation to a whole other way of communication. I think He is telling those of us who feel like prayer is a never-ending fight, *Go ahead and fight. But don't fight to achieve. Fight for peace to rule your heart. Fight off any voice that says you have to work your way to Me. Fight to make time with Me, so you feel a sense of My love for you. Fight off any thought or mind-set that would tell you I'm not always with and for you.* You see, we don't fight to pray in order to blackmail God. We don't pray to coerce or manipulate Him.

We don't fight to earn.

We don't fight *or* rest.

We fight *to* rest.

I used to be confused by two ideas in Scripture. In Psalm 46:10 we read, "Be still, and know that I am God." Yet Paul admonishes Timothy to "Fight the good fight of the faith" (1 Timothy 6:12). Well, which one is it? *God, are You asking me to be still or get up and take action? Do You want me to be at peace, or do You want me to take the kingdom by force?* Well, I believe it's both, not one or the other. We aren't resting and then fighting. We aren't fighting and then resting. We do one *for* the other. We fight *to rest* in the promises of God. We wrestle the lies and pin them down with the reality of the love of God. We are fighting to find rest for our souls in all we already have in Jesus.

We fight the lies, the need to be recognized, the fame mongering, and the endless suspicion that we aren't enough. But why? Why does it always feel like such a fight to rest? Well, I think there are plenty of reasons for that. For me, the main reason is this: before God made me to do anything for Him, He made me to be known by Him. I avoid it, though, because being busy is easier than being known. We want a life hack to peace, a shortcut to intimacy. There isn't one. The result is a hobbling humanity trying so desperately to get the rest that God is already freely offering to them. I've heard it said, "We're human beings, not human doings." That kind of sounds like a bumper sticker, but it's true. Perhaps this is why we are admonished in Scripture to pray continually. Prayer recenters us. It is God's gift to us, a way to step off the conveyor belt of life. It's a chance to remind ourselves of whose we are. We do not belong to our deadlines. We belong to Him.

Time to Be

Brennan Manning, whose books wrecked my limited views of God's kindness, said he used to pray one simple prayer for hours on end: "Abba, I belong to You." *Abba* was an Aramaic name for "father." He would even center his breathing on the phrase, an exercise that is sometimes called a breath prayer. He would say "Abba" on the in-breath and "I belong to You" on the out-breath. This practice helped Brennan find his purpose and comfort in being God's child.[3] To this day, I find myself repeating this prayer quietly in between chores and while waiting in lines. You and I must take time to do this. We need to just be, to rest in the work of God, and to let ourselves be known. Now, if you're a single parent or working several jobs to make ends meet, this might seem impractical. Time? Who has time? What is this time you speak of? It can seem impossible during stressful seasons, but we must make room to be with the Lord or we may run out of room for everyone around us. It can feel like a waste of time when priorities pile up, but it's strange how less stressful my to-do lists feel after I've sat in prayer, doing nothing but communing with the Almighty for a few moments first.

I have struggled to articulate the value of "wasting" time with God in prayer over the years. I specifically remember struggling to come up with a valid response during a meet and greet before a show in South Florida. I think it might have been ten years ago now, but I still remember the moment. The show was near the college from which we had just graduated, and there were several current students in line to meet me and the other band members.

One girl stared me dead in the eyes and asked, "Have you spent time with God today?" It was an interrogation. "What verses have you read?" She asked these questions with such quiet ferocity, I remember a tremble going through me.

"Um-m-m," I stammered, "I haven't read the Bible yet today, but I did take some time by the water over there to pray?" It sort of came out like a question.

She pounced. "That's extremely disappointing for someone who's going to be onstage here soon. You can't possibly have anything to share with us now."

Ouch. That stung deeply because, though she was half wrong, I knew she was also half right.

It's true that we can only share what we have ingested and marinated in. Aaron Weiss, who is the front man for the band mewithoutYou, wrote this line in a song by the same name, "A glass can only spill what it contains."[4] I agree wholeheartedly. I must be filled first, before I'm ready to give. This girl, as well intentioned as she may or may not have been, made an assumption quite common in our investment-savvy society. In our modern accomplishment-oriented culture, we describe our times with God by what we feel we got out of it. We put great stock in what God showed us and how strongly we felt His presence. Just as Henry Scougal so eloquently observed in his beautiful letter, *The Life of God in the Soul of Man,* "Others again put all religion in the affections, in rapturous hearts, and ecstatic devotion; and all they aim at is, to pray with passion, and to think of heaven with pleasure, and to be affected with those kind and melting expressions . . . till they persuade themselves they are mightily in love with him."[5] Scougal goes on to say that the chief goal of religion isn't about feelings but the fact that God has changed your soul.

We often think that if we don't feel tingly all over or cry hot tears during our times with God, then we probably did something wrong. We turn spiritual disciplines into performances. We quantify, evaluate, and track our progress. We prod one another by saying, "Did you *do* your devotions today?" or "Did you *spend* time with the Lord?" I believe this is a subversive and dangerous approach because we view our relationship with God as transactional. Have you thought about that? Isn't the word *spend* a consumeristic term? As if being with God were something we must do, as opposed to something we're invited into. It's a slippery slope when you begin to break down a living, breathing connection into bullet points and how-tos. Remember what Jesus said to Martha? "You are anxious and troubled about many things, but one thing is necessary. Mary has chosen the good portion" (Luke 10:41–42). He looked right into the eyes of Martha, the do-gooder, and He questioned her priorities. What did Mary do that Martha did not? She sat at Jesus's feet. She just sat there.

Like I said before, I'm not good at sitting still. To just sit down in front of Jesus and do nothing would probably demand I strait-jacket myself to His sandals. Regardless, prayerlessness is sin (see 1 Samuel 12:23). It's proclaiming you don't need assistance. If sin is building your life on something other than God, then living without prayer is defiance. It's asserting that you can live without Him. This is good news. It means prayer, then, is, in essence, nothing more than admitting your need.

All Prayer Is Need

I've heard it said you shouldn't go to God only when you need something, but I think I'm starting to disagree. Is it even possible to approach God without needing something? When do we not need something from Him? What else besides our needs do we ever bring Him? Let me try to unpack that, because you might argue that we must first come with adoration and thanksgiving. Question: Isn't gratitude the need to direct our attention on the One who is worthy of it? What is adoration except our need to be free from the slavery of self so we can revel in the limitless glory of God? If He gives to us life, breath, and all things, isn't need the only thing we ever bring to Him? If we think we go to God with more than need, aren't we bringing too much?

With this understanding, let's look at the Lord's Prayer in Matthew 6:9–13.

Pray then like this:

"Our Father in heaven,
hallowed be your name.
Your kingdom come,
your will be done,
    on earth as it is in heaven.
Give us this day our daily bread,
and forgive us our debts,
    as we also have forgiven our debtors.
And lead us not into temptation,
    but deliver us from evil."

Everything Jesus tells us to pray is a request. These requests can't be easily identified as adoration, confession, thanksgiving, then supplication. Everything comes down to our need. We need to remember whose we are by saying, "Our Father." We need to adore someone higher than ourselves: Our Father "in heaven." We need to realize this isn't our story, by saying, "Your kingdom come." We need to relinquish our plans for His: "Your will be done." We need to admit our needs, by asking, "give us this day our daily bread." We need to admit we're wrong: "forgive us our debts." We need to forgive others, "as we forgive others." We need deliverance: "deliver us from evil." We need direction for every step, asking, "lead us not into temptation." Never worry that you're bothering God with your needs. As the hymn "Come Ye Sinners" says, "All the fitness He requires is to feel your need of Him."[6]

Jesus demonstrated this for us with astonishing humility. He was not afraid to acknowledge His unending need for the Father's presence. Time and again Jesus walked away from the swarming throngs of people and sought out desolate places where He could be with His Father. He obviously found something in the Father's presence that He wasn't able to access in any other way. He knew where His help came from.

If we are to follow Jesus, then we must follow Him in this regard as well. If Jesus needed time with His Father, how much more do we? I don't know how or when you can carve out those times, but for me, time with God is oxygen for my works-infatuated, self-centered soul. And let me be clear. I don't want to paint some picture of my prayer life where I'm floating around playing a harp with a bunch of naked baby cherubim. Far from it. Prayer is almost always a struggle for me. It's like spotty cellular service, touch and go, often feeling more like an on-the-go snack than a five-course meal. I don't always feel like meditating on Scripture. I don't feel much of anything most of the time. Going to God in prayer doesn't always have an immediate effect. But I have to say, later—minutes, hours, sometimes days or months later—I notice an underlying peace I didn't have before. It's almost as if, when I allow God the space to speak—even if He doesn't—I feel a deeper peace knowing at least I gave Him the chance to.

Never Wasted Time

Jason, my longtime friend and former bandmate, stumbled across the following quote by Henri Nouwen the other day, and it has renewed my heart for prayer.

> My hour in the Carmelite chapel is more important than I can fully know myself. It is not an hour of deep prayer, nor a time in which I experience a special closeness to God; it is not a period of serious attentiveness to the divine mysteries. I wish it were! On the contrary, it is full of distractions, inner restlessness, sleepiness, confusion, and boredom. It seldom, if ever, pleases my senses. But the simple fact of being for one hour in the presence of the Lord and of showing him all that I think, feel, sense, and experience, without trying to hide anything, must please him. Somehow, somewhere, I know that he loves me, even though I do not feel that love as I can feel a human embrace, even though I do not hear a voice as I hear human words of consolation, even though I do not see a smile as I can see a human face. Still the Lord speaks to me, looks at me, and embraces me there, where I am still unable to notice it. The only way I become aware of his presence is in that remarkable desire to return to that quiet chapel and be there without any real satisfaction. . . . When I feel this inner pull to return again to that hidden hour of prayer, I realize that something is happening that

is so deep that it becomes like the riverbed through
which the waters can safely flow and find their way to
the open sea.[7]

These words have breathed new life and grace over my rest-less, poor, praying heart. I am also encouraged by Paul's wise words in Romans 8:26, "Likewise the Spirit helps us in our weak-ness. For we do not know what to pray for as we ought, but the Spirit himself intercedes for us with groanings too deep for words." So take heart, friend. You're not too needy for God. He isn't disap-pointed by your need for Him; He welcomes it. And if you strug-gle to pray, to keep quiet, and to tame your thoughts before God, know you're not alone. Know that it pleases our Father's heart even when we pray unsuccessfully. He gladly welcomes you, even when it feels like "wasting" time on Him. Time "wasted" on God is always time well spent.

Always Available Joy

The secret to joy is to keep seeking God
where we doubt He is.

—ANN VOSKAMP, ONE THOUSAND GIFTS

A s we follow Jesus into prayer, we may even find ourselves
stumbling into gratitude. The more we lay our need before
Him, the more we are able to recognize what He's doing
in our lives. In turn, we become more grateful, and gratitude then
gives birth to joy.

Of course, I believe the words "rejoice always" in 1 Thessalonians 5:16 are true and that it's always possible to find joy. However, we must hold those words in balance with the admonition to
"rejoice with those who rejoice, weep with those who weep" (Romans 12:15). Joy is always possible, but that doesn't mean we don't
make our way to gratitude slowly and through a valley of tears.

Did you see the Pixar movie *Inside Out*? I love the scene

where Sadness helps Riley feel better, and Joy understands how important that is.[1] Sometimes these emotions don't contradict each other but blend together to bring us a deeper sense of wholeness. One of my favorite Jars of Clay songs, "The Valley Song (Sing of Your Mercy)," soars, "I will sing of Your mercy that leads me through valleys of sorrow to rivers of joy."[2] Gratitude and joy are points on the compass we direct our ship toward. Our hearts were made to feel both of these emotions. But sometimes we must walk through chaos to get there. The calm after the storm brings another kind of peace all its own. I learned what that meant ten years ago.

The band and I were on our first national tour. After years of playing summer camps, youth lock-ins, and hole-in-the-wall venues, we had made the "big time." I put that in quotation marks because I've now realized there is no such thing. We were opening up for the well-established and much heralded CCM rock band, *Sanctus Real.* Kelly and I were newlyweds and lived in a five-hundred-square-foot apartment in the front half of a duplex. Our band had signed a record deal, and we had recently celebrated newfound radio success. However, we were still living paycheck to paycheck. In fact, financially we were barely scraping by. Up to that point, we had never done a traditional-style tour. We usually played retreats, camps, or special events, meaning we'd drive for a day or two, but then we'd have a couple of days to settle in and hang out. We had never performed in a different city every night for months on end. We were in for a rude awakening.

We spent three months following a tour bus in our fifteen-passenger van. If you've ever been in a band, you know the drill.

This is the rite of passage, as it were. I bought a little camping air mattress to wedge down on the floor between the bench and the two front captain seats. Even though the space was cramped, I honestly slept better on the floor, and I could even hold Kelly's hand while we slept. Aww. With her on the bench seat above and me on the floor below, we covered almost every inch of the American interstate system. Yeah, this was the "big time."

Far from Fabulous

A few weeks before the tour started, Kelly and I discovered we were pregnant. I was stoked for sure but also understandably scared out of my mind. I didn't even know how we were going to pay for gas to get to the next show, let alone how I was going to provide for a family. But we had committed to the tour and had no other plan in place, so with a baby in her belly and a cooler full of peanut butter and jelly sandwiches in the back of the van, we ventured out into the unknown world of full-time touring.

It was brutal.

Most nights we slept in the van. We followed the tour bus and became well acquainted with truck stops and bad coffee. Occasionally we could afford a luxury—maybe Starbucks or Subway— but those nights were rare. Imagine living a sort of glorified "homeless" lifestyle. Sleeping on floors but getting applauded for thirty minutes every night. It was a strange reality. Mostly, we slogged through, running on copious amounts of caffeine and sleep-deprived delirium. Our coworkers at our new record label assured us things were going to get better. "Just you wait," they would say. "Things will be so much different come this time next year!" It turned out they were right, but I didn't believe them. We had songs topping the charts on national radio stations, and our records were supposedly being purchased by people we didn't know all across the country. But truthfully, we felt far from popular and more impoverished than ever.

One night three weeks into tour, Kelly whispered to me from the bench above. "Something's wrong." She was bleeding, which is not a good sign early in a pregnancy. My hands tingled. Time stood still. My face went pale. We were in the middle of an all-night drive to Colorado. We stopped at an ER in Kansas City. Hours later, in a cold and sterile examination room, a nurse flatly told us, "I can't find a heartbeat."

Our heads spun. Our hearts sank. "Are you sure?" We choked back tears.

"I don't know," she responded. "We can't tell you anything at this point. There could be plenty of reasons I can't find it. I'm sure everything is fine. There are no signs you'll lose the baby."

We pressed her for more answers. "Then why is she bleeding? Why does it feel like something's not right?"

She simply looked at us and told us we could pay at the front. To make matters worse, we couldn't do anything but keep driving. After singing the next night in what felt like a numbing fog, we set off for our next show. Two more weeks of tour passed, but I don't recall much of it. What I do remember is huddling with my sweet wife under the privacy of a blanket on the van's front bench, weeping together until there were no tears left.

When we arrived in Northern California, her pain increased,

and despite our prayers and pleas with God to heal our baby, we feared the worst. We made another hospital visit in Santa Ana, but this time it was as if God Himself personally trained the entire staff. A nurse bearing sleeve tattoos stopped and prayed with us. Several nurses who weren't assigned to us stopped in to offer empathy and asked if there was anything they could do. A kind and gracious doctor, whose name I've sadly forgotten, came in shortly after we arrived. He gently and compassionately broke the news to us that Kelly was in the beginning stages of a miscarriage.

Miscarriage. Though we suspected it was coming, it was the first time we had heard the word, and it hit us with hammer-like force.

Even though it happens more than most realize, it's just not a word you're ready to have in your vocabulary. We sat in a daze for what felt like hours and let the news slowly sink in. But even in that moment, we were overwhelmed by the startlingly different attitude and love of the doctors at this hospital. In the very moment we were crying out to God, asking, "Where are You?" those doctors and nurses in that California hospital were His very hands and feet to us. To this day, I thank God for dressing up in blue scrubs and caring for us through them.

Wrecked, poor, and not sure of what to do next, we mechanically discussed our options. Do we stay here? Do we fly home? Do we cancel the tour? Unsure of how soon Kelly would lose the baby, and lacking the means to do anything about it, we drove on to the next city. We staggered into the venue sometime in the afternoon and were met with even more compassion. The boys in Sanctus Real heard what was happening and graciously bought Kelly a plane ticket home. We were beyond relieved. The only problem was that it was already too late to get a flight out that night, so we had to drive through the night yet again to get her to LAX the next morning.

We arrived at five o'clock in the morning, three hours before her departure time. At this point, she was cramping badly, and I was growing increasingly anxious. She was miraculously calm. She held my face in her hands and assured me she was going to be all right. I remember how impossibly steady her hands were. Mine wouldn't stop shaking.

She had spoken to God the night before, she told me. He had told her that this baby was going to be home with Him. She also had been singing the words of the Sanctus Real song "Whatever You're Doing (Something Heavenly)" to herself. I had heard them sing it every night of the tour, yet the words didn't really hit me until that moment: "Whatever you're doing inside of me, it feels like chaos but somehow there's peace, and though it's hard to surrender to what I can't see, I'm giving in to something heavenly."[3]

We had to leave her at seven, and somewhere around seven fifteen, I received this text: "I passed the baby in the toilet. I held him in my hands and thanked God for his life. I know he's home now."

Even as I type this, I'm choking back tears. Ten years have passed, and I still can't tell you why our baby went home to heaven so soon. I also can't tell you why Kelly is certain it was a boy. But I can tell you, inexplicably, we experienced a supernatural peace that transcended understanding. Philippians 4:4, 6–7 has some insight on the matter:

Rejoice in the Lord always; again I will say, rejoice. . . .
Do not be anxious about anything, but in everything
by prayer and supplication with thanksgiving let your
requests be made known to God. And the peace of God,
which surpasses all understanding, will guard your hearts
and your minds in Christ Jesus.

It's still a mystery to me, but this was one time that I saw this play out in real life. We thanked God for our baby's life. We thanked Him for the hospital staff. We thanked Him for all the kindness that was shown to us through so many people. We didn't get the answers we wanted, but we did receive the peace that we needed.

I want to add that I do not believe our baby died because we didn't have enough faith. I cling to the belief that what matters most isn't how much faith we have but who our faith is in. I believe we should never stop praying for and expecting miracles, but we should also keep believing God is good, even if we don't see a miracle.

I've even heard Todd White, who has become renowned for healing and miracles, say, "I have seen stuff not work out the way God says it would, but I'm not going to take my experience and rise it above what God's Word says. I'm not telling you it feels good. It doesn't feel good."[4]

That might sound strong, but I think it's beautiful. This type of thinking allows me to sit in the mystery that our God, the creator of life, allows death. I don't have to think that God wanted my baby to die. Rather, I can go on thanking God for my child's life, however brief, and thank Him for allowing my child to be in heaven. I can leave it at that.

I think it's okay to refrain from developing theology when God stays silent. Where God speaks, we speak. What He leaves a mystery, maybe we should too. It's okay not to have answers. Answers have rarely ever changed a heart. But a moment of knowing God is near, especially in the midst of pain, can set your heart on a new course.

Peace is still possible. It's possible to hate sickness and not curse God at the same time. It's possible to say, "I trust you, God," while also crying honestly, "I don't know why this happened." In our hardest moments, we can keep giving thanks for life while we go on hating death. I think God hates death too.

Gratitude Readies Us for Heartbreak

Being joyful in all things doesn't mean there is an absence of sorrow. Likewise, courage is not the absence of fear. There aren't always answers for tragedy. I cringe when someone is speaking at a funeral and says, "I know it was God's will to bring them home." I've heard all the arguments on both sides, but I don't believe we have to tidy up our grief. Yes, we should be glad our loved one is home in heaven, but maybe we aren't ready to celebrate it just yet. Maybe it's okay to grieve what we've lost. If Jesus wept at His friend Lazarus's tomb, then I think He'd understand when we cry at our loved ones' funerals too.

When Jesus hung on the cross, He cried out with His last breaths, "My God, my God, why have you forsaken me?" (Mark

15:34). Doesn't that seem to tell us, *Even in your confusion, even in your questions, I am there! I, too, hate death, and when you feel like the Father has left you, take heart; I've felt that too*? I don't think you and I will ever comprehend why some people are healed and others aren't, at least not this side of heaven. But I can tell you this: There is a supernatural grace to help us give thanks in all circumstances. It's possible. The Holy Spirit is far more powerful than we give Him credit for. He is able to comfort us. He is able to lessen the sting of loss with His sweetness. In our simple act of giving thanks, not only do we protect our hearts from the danger of ingratitude, but we also open ourselves up to the presence of God.

Gratitude is a shield protecting our hearts from bitterness. I've seen it in my own life over and over. When I do not stop to name the blessings in my life or express my thankfulness, I eventually feel entitled. In essence, the act of giving thanks is like armor we put around our hearts, protecting us from feeling like God owes us something. In that sense, gratitude readies us for heartbreak. It loosens our iron grip on that which was never ours to keep in the first place. This reminds me of how A. W. Tozer described Abraham in *The Pursuit of God*. After Abraham took Isaac up on the mountainside to sacrifice him in obedience to God, he was a changed man. He may have gone up the mountain clinging to his son and the promise he represented, but coming down the mountain, he had far more than he went up with. Abraham came down with the "blessedness of possessing nothing."[5]

Thanksgiving is the gate that opens onto our path to joy. Through thanksgiving, we can find joy in the midst of our suffering. To praise God in the middle of heartbreak is to begin to find nourishment in trusting Him. Giving thanks means clinging to hope when all hope seems to be lost. It means accepting that this world is not as it should be but one day all will be well. One day, God will make everything right, and all that is sad will come untrue. In the meantime, giving thanks is surrendering our demands and our need for things to go our way. That's why thanksgiving is a sacrifice (see Psalm 50:23). We are putting our will on the altar and choosing to let go of the belief that God can't redeem what we're walking through. We let go of the assumption that God got it wrong or the suffocating suspicion that He won't get it right. To say "thank you" is to surrender control.

My friend Daniel's church just did a series on a similar idea. They called it "It's Just a Phase." The preachers talked about how so many of us say to one another, "It's just a phase. You'll get through it." But we ought to say, "It's just a phase. Don't miss it." Often we're so concerned with changing the outcome of what we're going through, or having our pain relieved, we tend to miss the supernatural healing God is offering us. We miss the words of Paul in 2 Corinthians 1:3–4, "Blessed be the . . . God of all comfort, who comforts us in all our affliction, so that we may be able to comfort those who are in any affliction, with the comfort with which we ourselves are comforted by God."

Good Friday Was the Worst Friday

In some supernatural place, Kelly was able to thank God when we lost our first child. I can only assume she found the strength to do so in knowing God, too, had lost a child. He knew exactly how she felt. Have you considered this in the pain of your own story? When disaster strikes, we can so quickly react by asking, "Why would a good God let bad things happen to good people?" when maybe we should marvel at the fact that a good God has allowed Himself to feel our pain.

On Good Friday, our Father in heaven delivered a death blow to the "bad things happen to good people" rhetoric. In light of the Cross, God can respond, *Why do you call Good Friday* good? *Good Friday wasn't the day a bad thing happened to a good person; it was the day the worst things happened to the best person, and you call it good?* Most of us would barely blink. For some reason or another, we can accept Jesus walking through the fire of the crucifixion, but we are confounded when God asks us to do the same.

And yes, we do live on the other side of Easter. We live in the reality that Jesus bore abuse and beatings so we could be healed and that He died to give us life. We live in the revelation of sin atoned for and our Messiah's victory over the curse. But why aren't we nervous when we read of Christ's unthinkable march toward death? Why do we scoff at the disciples' unbelief as they scattered and ran? "Don't they know what's happening?" we cry. "Don't they remember Jesus saying He'd rise again? Don't they know it's all gonna be all right?"

It's amazing what we can understand in hindsight, isn't it? With the clarity of distance, we know the answers to God's questions. Good Friday is good because Sunday came! We can see grace in both triumph and tragedy. Maybe it's the same for you and me. In this life or the next, we'll be able to look back on certain "worst Fridays" of our own and see God was up to something beautiful, even then. Maybe one day all our worst Fridays will be good Fridays because we'll see them against the backdrop of God's kingdom come. I won't lie, though. It's not usually the Fridays when I lose hope. It's the Saturdays. Saturday is the day in between. It's the day of waiting. It's the day when hope wears thin, and the cynics seem correct. I've often been confounded by the fact that Jesus felt the need to be dead until Sunday.

I'm sure there is a lot of cultural and historical relevance here. I know the Jews didn't consider you fully dead until the third day,[6] but I can't help but think, *Why couldn't Jesus have just been dead till Saturday? Why did God make the disciples wait that whole extra day?* Why make us wait in the middle of our suffering? Last Easter, as I was reading and questioning, it was almost as if God was calling out to me from the pages of the Bible.

Don't you see, My child? You're not the only one who has walked through Saturdays. You're not the only one who's felt the waiting's gone on too long. You're not alone in your longing for redemption. You're not alone in your questions, in your hopelessness, in your doubts. You're not too worn out, even on your worst Friday. You're not alone, even as you walk through Easter Saturdays. Give Me enough time, and I will make even these days good.

Romans 8:18 says, "The sufferings of this present time are not worth comparing with the glory that is to be revealed to us." How would it change the way we follow God through tragedy if we really believed the best is yet to come? What if we believed, however fragile the belief, that God was really able to redeem all things into something good? I mean, if He was able to work salvation for the human race out of the worst day in human history, then maybe—just maybe—He can bring something beautiful out of the chaos of our lives.

When our first daughter was born a year later, there were simultaneous tears of joy and tears of sorrow. But the pain of love was worth it. The pain of trust and the sacrifice of praise were enough to break down the dangerous walls of bitterness that so easily could have built up around my heart. I pray I can remember this more often. No matter how hard it is, I don't want to be one of the nine lepers who didn't think to praise God (Luke 17:11–19). To quote the song "Even When It Hurts (Praise Song)" by Hillsong United: "Even when it hurts like hell, I'll praise you." It was no coincidence that on that same tour, I came across some of my favorite words in all of literature. In Fyodor Dostoyevsky's novel *The Brothers Karamazov,* the following words shone brighter than my best attempts to sum up my thoughts:

> I believe like a child that suffering will be healed and made up for, that all the humiliating absurdity of human contradictions will vanish like a pitiful mirage . . . in the world's finale, at the moment of eternal harmony, something so precious will come to pass that it will suffice for all hearts, for the comforting of all resentments, for the atonement of all the crimes of humanity, for all the blood that they've shed; that it will make it not only possible to forgive but justify all that has happened.[7]

My church has a beautiful tradition each Easter weekend. At the beginning of the Good Friday silent service, they hand out three-inch nails to every congregant. As we sit there in hushed reverence, feeling the cold steel in our hands, engrossed by the inevitable clang of a mishandled nail dropping against the cement floor, the haunting echoes resurrect haunting memories of our own mishandling. Readings and musical interludes follow, but no words are ever spoken by congregants. The hour-long service concludes with an invitation to walk to the front of the church, where we hammer our nails and regrets to the cross before receiving communion. The sound of hammers on metal is a fitting soundtrack as we admit our part in our Lord's gruesome demise.

On Easter morning, we are greeted with a new visceral experience. The cross that bore all our nails just two days before has been placed at the front of the church. As the worship team erupts into praise, every child in the church is handed fistfuls of bright yellow flowers. As the music crescendos, kids race to the cross to place their bouquets in the holes the nails left behind. It's a stunning and incendiary visual for gratitude. Those flaming bright petals remind me that suffering and death are making room for the birth of new life.

I want to give thanks in every season because I believe the places where the nails were driven deepest are the same places a future flower's roots can grow the deepest. Something far more beautiful than a hundred daisies is coming. The realization that we will one day see true beauty face to face not only makes it possible to get through our tragedies but also enables us to thank God for them. We already do it every Easter, don't we? We thank God for Good Friday. In doing so, we testify that His greatest tragedy was our greatest victory.

13

Living the Perpetual Yes

After the final no there comes a yes.
And on that yes the future world
depends.

—WALLACE STEVENS,
"THE WELL DRESSED MAN WITH A BEARD"

I f you ever want to feel gratitude, peace, or joy, you have to start with the word *yes*. Of all the words in the English language, *yes* has to be the one with the most letter-to-power ratio. What a word! It's so short and so common, yet beyond it lies the entire mysterious force of our lives. Gratitude begins with saying yes to what God has allowed to happen in the past. Peace comes by saying yes to what God is allowing in the present. Joy and passion are merely the robust by-products when we say yes to whatever God has planned for the future. Gratitude, peace, and joy all begin with yes.

Just the other day, saying yes got me right up next to joy. Literally. Her name was Joy. She was sitting in the very last row of a Southwest flight I was taking to play a concert in Sacramento. I almost didn't sit next to her. I don't know if you know how the Southwest seating system works, but there are no assigned seats. You board the plane in order of your boarding group and position, and seats are first come, first served. Since I was one of the first ten people on the plane, I had eagerly snatched up a lovely aisle seat in the fourth row. The guy sitting by the window had his bag in the middle seat, hoping to create the working man's first-class situation. I didn't mind. I was right up front, ready to jump off once we landed, and more importantly on a four-hour flight, close to the bathroom. Then the inconvenient voice of God started speaking, and I couldn't ignore Him.

God's voice started on the intercom: "Ladies and gentlemen, we have a completely full flight. Every seat will be taken. Go ahead and remove any bags you've placed trying to save those seats." The guy next to me groaned as he slid his bag down to the floor. As the masses boarded group by group, the entire plane filled up to overflowing until an elderly woman and her forty-something-year-old son were the last two standing. They stood bewildered next to me. There were only two open seats left on the entire vessel, and one was the middle seat next to me. They didn't understand the system. "Where are we going to sit?" She sounded distraught. "I don't know, Mama!" he replied with gritted teeth, quelling a growl.

God came to their aid by inconveniencing me. *Give them your seat, Mike.*

"No, God. This is why I checked in early. Serves them right for not adequately preparing."

Is that the way I work, Mike?

"Shut up, God. I'm tired."

Miiiiike . . .

I finally caved. I let the woman into the second to last open seat next to me and pried myself out of mine. I begrudgingly chased the son to the very last row, to the very last seat on the plane. "You can have my seat," I squeaked out through a fake smile. "It would be my honor," I lied.

"Oh thanks, man." He galumphed his way past me to the front of the plane, where the passengers had begun high-fiving and throwing confetti. I couldn't be sure, but they may have even been handing out gold bars. It didn't matter. I was no longer part of the front-of-plane party. I slouched into the middle seat in the very last row. My seat didn't recline because it hit up against the bathroom wall. I was already regretting my decision. I settled in amid a choir of babies' screams. "Why are we surrounded by so many children and so much agony?" I lamented under my breath.

"Did you give up your seat for that fella? That sure was sweet of ya!" A lilting voice floated beside me. I turned my head to meet the eyes of a dolled-up seventy-six-year-old woman who I could tell had personality to spare. Joy launched right into her story, and five minutes later, I was already repenting nearly missing the opportunity to meet her.

"I wrote a book," she told me once I told her what I was

working on. "It's called *Imprisoned with Jesus*. I was wrongfully imprisoned for three years for something my husband did. Best thing that ever happened to me. . . . Close your mouth, dear."

My gaping mouth probably resembled that of a largemouth bass. "Best thing that ever happened to you? Tell me more!" I finally managed to say.

She told me her whole life story. She told me about the time the warden took her out to a steak and lobster dinner. She told me how she was given favor with the guards. She told me how God protected her from another inmate who was threatening her. She teared up as she recounted the time hundreds of butterflies landed on her as she stepped into the prison yard one day. She told me how often she had read the book of Job and how she knew beyond a shadow of a doubt that there are no chance meetings. I had to agree with her. When I told her I was working on a chapter about saying yes, she chuckled and handed me her drink napkin. It read, "In a world full of no, we're a plane full of yes."

I'm pretty sure Joy was an angel, the kind that wears red lipstick and cowboy boots and laughs about going to prison. I told her how I'd seen a *20/20* special Diane Sawyer once did on women's prisons in America and how they showed a women's prison choir singing our song, "Worn." She thought that was the greatest thing she'd ever heard.

She told me how, like Joseph in the book of Genesis, she was wrongly imprisoned, but also like him, she eventually learned to say of her incarcerators, "What some meant for evil, God means for good." She went on, "Sweetie, that's for certain. My husband was killed by drug dealers while I was in jail. God put me away in a safe place for three years, where no one could get me, and that's the truth. You know, Mike . . . Is your name Mike or Michael? . . . Oh. I had a son named Michael . . . The quicker you accept where you are, the clearer you'll be able to see where you're going."

I'm so glad I said yes to inconvenience on that plane. I would have completely missed the opportunity to hear Joy's stories. I even looked up her book later and never found it, which only seems to confirm my suspicion she was an actual angel. It didn't take much. But I believe our ability to see God at work always begins with the smallest and simplest of responses. Just like Joy going to prison or like me moving to the back of the plane (admittedly much less serious). I asked Joy for writing advice, and she simply said, "Listen to God. And when you don't know where to go, stand." I love that. Listen to God, wait for a word. Stand, and when He asks something of you, just say yes. The life He has waiting for us always begins with that beautiful three-letter word.

Keep Saying Yes

My life of full-time touring started the same way. Long before we signed a record deal, our band had been touring the country in that glorious fifteen-passenger van I mentioned earlier. I should reiterate that calling it touring might be a little bit of an overstatement. This was long before we had a record deal and before our songs were getting radio play. Again, way before we started playing in a different city every day and before anyone knew or cared who our band was. You could say we were much less like worship leaders and more like worship paupers. This is an aside, but I can't tell you how many times I wished we hadn't named our band after the street we lived on in college. Some yeses are a bit premature. If we knew it was going to become our career, we would have put a lot more thought into it. Without fail, each new youth pastor would butcher our name as he introduced us to his church group. "All right, kids, here they are"—awkward moment of silence— "Sixth . . . Street . . . Southwest!" (Our actual band name is Tenth Avenue North, but it didn't really matter.)

Time changed things, and we've gone on to playing bigger shows and rooms and crowds, but it all began with a yes. My friend Clint asked me if I wanted to jam with his roommate who played drums. I said yes. The next day a classmate of mine asked me to play at a school coffeehouse. I said yes. The next year our friends Salina and Joseph asked us to join them at a weekend Cru conference. Six months later, Andrew Oates asked us to be the worship team for the high school youth group. Then we received a call to play at our first summer camp. Another yes. A church leader at the camp asked us to play at another camp. You see where this is going. A sweet sixteen party, an assisted living home, a service for deaf people. . . . The list grew and grew, and before we knew it, we were in the midst of a full-time operation.

From Wednesday night youth group gigs to weekend trips, our travel time increased by days and then weeks until we were leaving home for months at a time. There was always lots of driving, lots of camps, and lots of bologna. SO. MUCH. BOLO-GNA. I daresay it was an absurd amount of bologna. Nay, an ungodly amount of bologna. And not just any bologna! Oh no! We're talking Gwaltney thick-sliced bologna. We hadn't yet gotten where we dreamed of going, but we weren't where we started. This life definitely wasn't glamorous, but it wasn't boring either. In those early days, when I had no family to serve or wife to care for, God gave me a never-ending green light. The best part? Saying yes to every opportunity gave me a whole different outlook about being onstage. Most groups we played for had no idea who we were or, for that matter, why we were there. Saying yes early on taught me I wasn't showing up to be served onstage. I was there to serve the people with the stage.

I kept saying yes. It changed me. One gig led to the next. One group led to the next group. Just the other day, while I was backstage at a festival, someone asked me, "How do I promote my artist?"

"That's the wrong question, I think," I responded. "Who is your artist trying to serve? Identify that first. It seems there's no shortage of opportunity when you're trying to serve people." There's no shortage of opportunity when you start saying yes to the opportunities right in front of you.

Learning to say yes eventually changed my songwriting, too. Admittedly, it wasn't as quick a change as I would have liked. But God's ways are often much slower and more meandering than we'd like, aren't they? We want highways or interstates. Get me from point A to point B as quickly as possible. As if life were a road trip with a friend who's up for anything, God often seems to take us on the backroads. We want the shortcut, and He wants us to enjoy the scenery. Songwriting came only when I was willing to hold God's hands as He led me along the crooked cliff paths. It came slowly, painstakingly slow.

When we weren't playing music at our church or driving somewhere a few states away, I spent days huddled in my room, working on getting better at the guitar and trying to figure out how to write songs. I had witnessed the power of songs in unforgettable ways. I had seen songs break chains of guilt, self-torment, and pride, just to name a few things. The problem was I was miles from knowing how to write what people would call "a good song." In fact, after about a hundred attempts, I still had failed to write a song that didn't make me nauseous when I listened to it. I dreamed of writing a song someone would want to hear more than once. What it would be like to write a song and have someone say, "I want to hear that again!" All the power I had witnessed through music came from playing other people's songs. Which, I might add, is amazing in and of itself, but I couldn't help but think there was something worth singing locked deep inside me too. I kept at it.

Then I stumbled across Psalm 49:4: "I will incline my ear to a proverb; I will solve my riddle to the music of the lyre." This gave me a new direction. Perhaps song writing was simply a gift I should use for my own personal and spiritual enrichment. Instead of writing a song for other people, what if I wrote simply to figure out where I was saying no to God? Where did God and I disagree? Perhaps I could start there. Like the psalmist, I would listen to wisdom. I would let His wisdom confront my foolishness, and with my music, I would let the Spirit unriddle my heart. Song writing suddenly felt more like free therapy sessions. I began wrestling with Scripture and with questions big and small. I still have to shake my head when I consider the songs God let me be a part of through that process.

"No" Is Interference

I quickly realized that "no" was the source of the interference. Previously, I wasn't hearing ideas for songs because the song could only start from the places where I began to say yes. Once I began bringing everything I was feeling to God, He began pointing out where I had gone wrong. This changed everything. Songs began to flow because I was always finding new places where I had, unbeknownst to even myself, told God no.

Not to be overly simplistic, but since that moment, I've come to believe almost all my problems begin with the equally powerful word *no*. Whether it's "No, I won't move forward until You give me all the facts" or "No, I will not follow You into forgiving that person." There's a plethora of little ways we say no to God every day. For me, I missed out on real songs, and the real life God had for me, when I simply shut down what He was asking of me in any particular moment. There is another way, and it begins in the tension between those simple but mighty words of *yes* and *no*.

Isn't that what the tree of the knowledge of good and evil is all about? God tells Adam and Eve (though not in so many words), "See that tree? I'm gonna give you freedom to choose between what I say is true and what you feel is true. But when you start switching names on that fruit, when you want to decide yes and no for yourself, when you want to disagree with how I think you should do things, trust me, all hell will break loose." Conversely, when we let God rename what's right and wrong, when we come into alignment with Him, things start to look a lot more like that perfect garden we're told about. The power of the choice between yes and no is like the power of creating heaven or creating hell. A simple yes to God is like rebuilding Eden. I tell that to my daughters when I drop them off for school. "Remember, girls, today you're bringing heaven to your elementary school." One yes at a time, we bring heaven to earth, until we suddenly find we're living the perpetual yes in His continual presence.

Say Yes to Doubt

When I wonder what it's like to live the perpetual yes, I think of Mary, the mother of Jesus. In the first chapter of Luke, an angel appeared to Mary and told her she was going to give birth to the Messiah. Although she was probably confused and distressed, Mary wondered, "'How will this be? . . .' And the angel answered her, 'The Holy Spirit will come upon you. . . . For nothing will be impossible with God.'" We hold our breath. In reply to this unthinkable proclamation, Mary said, "Let it be to me according to your word." (Luke 1:34–38).

Unbelievable.

Mary, in spite of her confusion and unanswered questions, including the potential threat of being stoned for becoming pregnant before she was married, embraced the perpetual yes and submitted her will to the life of God. I can't even imagine that sort of radical obedience. Of all the things to marvel at Mary for, this has to top the list. A teenage girl surrenders her life before the unthinkable command of her Lord. May we all learn to follow her in this way.

But there's something even stranger about this story. A few verses earlier, we read the story of Zechariah, who was the father of John the Baptist. He also received word from an angel that a miraculous conception had taken place. His wife, Elizabeth, old and barren though she was, was going to give birth to a son. But what's weirder than this is how Zechariah seems to answer the angel in much the same way Mary did, yet he is met with a vastly different outcome. "How shall I know this? For I am an old man, and my wife is advanced in years" (Luke 1:18). Sounds just like Mary, right? That's what I always thought. Except after his questions, Zechariah wasn't lauded and blessed like Mary but instead cursed with muteness! Now, what's the deal, God? Why can Mary have questions but he can't?

When I was on staff at the church, my mentor, Andrew, helped me understand the subtle but significant difference in their questioning. In a sermon to a group of college students, Andrew said, "There can be miles of difference in the heart of our questioning. It seems to me Mary questioned to truly understand, while Zachariah questioned to further his doubt." I agree with him now. It's a subtle but dynamic delineation. I suppose you could call it the difference between scoffing and inquiry. Though they look the same on paper, they are radically different matters of the heart.

In other words, say yes to doubt. Say yes to all, even when you don't understand. Say yes to your questions, but let there be a yes residing underneath those questions. Think of it as a willingness to trust the heart of God. Our trust in the bizarre and beautiful guidance of God will require us to humbly accept that we won't always have every answer. Even years later, I often call to mind Andrew's words. It's beautiful to know that living a perpetual yes doesn't mean I can't have questions. It doesn't mean I can't have doubt. Rather, it means I need to keep bringing my doubt boldly before the throne of God. While skeptics argue with one another, the children of God have the privilege of bringing their arguments to the Father. There are no questions we cannot bring when they are brought with a heart of humility.

Jonah Versus Job

I suppose this is the question we're perpetually asking: What if I keep saying yes to doubt and yes to what I think God wants, but things keep getting worse? How long do I hold out hope for the girl when we've broken up? How long do I keep going in my career when I'm surviving on lines of credit and it looks like my dream is dead? How do I know when God's telling me I should say yes to a different direction? I call questions like these Jonah versus Job questions. When everything falls apart, is it because we're like Jonah running from the Lord's command, or because we're like Job enduring a difficult trial? Is this a sovereignly appointed valley I'm being led through, or am I just an idiot? Is this the natural consequences of running in the wrong direction?

I was standing at the bathroom mirror recently, and the word *bitterness* came to mind. If you go back and read the stories of

Jonah and Job, you'll see they had vastly different heart positions. They both went through hell and back, and at first blush it's easy to assume that Job went through hell because God wanted him to, while Jonah went through hell because he was a moron. I don't think it's that simple, though. Could it be there's a simple attitude adjustment God wanted us to see in these scriptural accounts? Job's friends seemed to be scratching their heads, wondering why he didn't just curse God and die. I mean, his situation was as awful as you can get. His cattle died, all his possessions were stolen, and then his house fell on all his children and killed them. I don't know. Seems like the guy must have gone way off track to deserve all that. On the other hand, the Lord called Jonah to preach the good news to an entire people group, but instead he ran the other way, climbed on a boat, and got tossed overboard. Even when a whale spit him up on dry land, he was still too bitter to allow repentance to happen. When God told him to go to Nineveh again, Jonah was incredulous. I know this because when Jonah finally preached to the people there, they repented and instead of marveling at God's goodness, Jonah was furious. He screamed at the Almighty, "That is why I made haste to flee to Tarshish; for I knew that you are a gracious God and merciful" (Jonah 4:2).

Oh, man. This hits me right between the eyes. Job, though he questioned God and at times was bitter in spirit, refused to make God his enemy. Jonah cursed God because God showed the Ninevites the same mercy He'd shown to Jonah. Next time chaos hits and I'm not sure how much longer I'm supposed to walk in what feels like the wrong direction, instead of questioning, maybe I simply need to ask whose heart I have. Despite all the death and loss and bewilderment Job endured, he did not call God out. Meanwhile, Jonah was so consumed by bitterness that he not only ran from God but blasted Him for being loving!

Hundreds of years later, Jesus warned us against living like Jonah. "If you do not forgive others their trespasses, neither will your Father forgive your trespasses" (Matthew 6:15). He was saying the only thing keeping us from forgiveness is our own unwillingness to forgive. Interesting, then, that God answers Jonah's indignation with a simple question: "Do you do well to be angry?" (Jonah 4:4).

What a question! I'm going to try that on my four-year-old next time she flings a memory game card across the room. "My child, do you do well to be angry?" I don't know if that would fly with her since she'd probably fling the next card at my nose, but it certainly is a much different way of addressing anger. We all want to know where God's path is, but meanwhile God is asking where our hearts are. "Do you do well to be angry?" He prods. "Are you angry with the way your life has gone? Are you mad things didn't go your way? Are you angry that I would bless someone who deserves it less than you? How is all that bitterness working out for you?"

But I'm learning. I'm learning! I'm learning all the time how to say yes to my wife and to my kids. I'm learning to say yes to serving every single minute. Ironically, this means I have to say no to a great deal of other things. This takes quite a bit of heart attention, because my perpetual yes to God means I will have to say no to a myriad of good things. Whenever we say yes to one thing, we're saying no to something else. If I had to choose, I'd say I should prioritize my yeses in God and my family's favor.

If I have to tell someone no, I pray it isn't God. As I said, without grace this is not just hard but downright impossible. Grace, though. Grace has repeatedly shown me how to calm down and engage every moment. Grace shows me how to stay when bitterness tells me to run. Grace, after all, is the belief that I'm always being treated better than I deserve. So then, grace shows me how to trust despite my questions. Grace shows me that more often than not, the hard thing is usually the right thing. And the right thing is as simple as saying yes where there was no. All God wants is me and my yes. Yes to Him. Yes to my wife. Yes to the present. When it comes to the life God is offering, may there never be a no in me and only a resounding and ever-cascading yes. Can that get exhausting? You'd better believe it. But when I teeter on the edge of burning out, shutting down, and coming back with an exuberant NO!, I find myself pausing to reflect on how Jesus never stops saying yes to me.

14

Drink the Cup

As they were eating, Jesus took bread,
and after blessing it broke it and gave it to
the disciples, and said, "Take, eat; this is
my body." And he took a cup, and when
he had given thanks he gave it to them,
saying, "Drink of it, all of you, for this is my
blood of the covenant, which is poured
out for many for the forgiveness of sins."
—MATTHEW 26:26–28

This is why Jesus says yes to us. He says yes to us when we throw a hand in His face. He says yes to us when we run the other way. He says yes to us because He wants to marry us. I know that sounds really strange, but it's true. Throughout the Old Testament, we see the prophets reminding God's people of His provision and love, warning them not to worship false gods.

Ezekiel scolded Israel for running after other lovers (Ezekiel 16). In the book of Isaiah we read, "As the bridegroom rejoices over the bride, so shall your God rejoice over you" (62:5). We even see this marriage language in the New Testament. Paul called the church God's bride in his letter to the Ephesians (5:24–29). Jesus Himself, at the last supper, in celebration of the Passover, presented His most shocking of all requests while holding a cup of wine: "Drink of it, all of you, for this is my blood of the covenant, which is poured out for many for the forgiveness of sins" (Matthew 26:27–28).

Now, it's difficult for us to hear the scandal of these words, and they certainly don't sound anything like wedding vows, because we hear them through our contemporary Western filter. We hear grape juice, wine, and wafers. But the disciples? They heard, "Will you marry me?"

First-Century Weddings

I was reading and researching the Last Supper some years ago and came across a man named Ray Vander Laan. He's the founder of That the World May Know ministries and a religion instructor in Michigan who has spent a large part of his life studying and teaching Jewish culture.[1] He helped me see the provocative nature of Jesus's request. Let me try to unpack some of what I learned from him.

In the time and culture in which Jesus lived, when a man wanted to marry a woman, he would say something similar to Jesus's words to the disciples. The man would go to his dad and say, "Yo, Pops. See that girl over there? I want to start a family with her. How do we get married?"

Next, his dad would approach the girl's dad and together they would agree upon a bride price, the payment from the groom's family to the potential bride's family. This payment was a way to ask her permission. She could say no if she wanted, because the payment was only buying the opportunity to ask—not the bride herself. The marriage wasn't yet a done deal. She had to be cool with it. "No way; you smell like hummus," she could have retorted.

You get the picture. If they agreed on a bride price—let's say, fifty camels—the groom would sit down with the aforementioned young woman and, with friends and family all watching, he would present his request to her. It was very unlikely she would say no, but it was a possibility. So he would fill a cup with wine and slide it across the table, saying, "This is my covenant with you. Take and drink." If she chose to refuse him, she could slide the cup right back to him, but if she was saying yes, she would pick up the cup and take a long, purposeful drink from the covenantal wine.

At this point, her name would change. During the engagement period, which could be as long as six months or a year, she would not be referred to by her name. She would be called One Who Was Bought with a Price. Meanwhile, she would return to her town, and the groom would go back to his. Chances are they didn't live anywhere close to one another, so they probably wouldn't see each other for the entire engagement. In fact, the only way they could communicate was through the best man. He served as a real-life text messenger, running back and forth with notes like, "Okay, this is what she says: check *yes, no,* or *maybe.*" The bride and the groom would not speak to each other or even see each other's faces until the wedding. On top of that, they also didn't know when the marriage ceremony would take place.

In effect, the man had to earn his marriage. He stayed at home working on the family *insula,* a collection of additions making up one sprawling house that could eventually take up an entire block. The insula was added onto, one relative at a time, year after year, marriage after marriage. Each time a new family member was betrothed, he set to work on his mansion. "A mansion?" You might have perked up at that word. Before you get too excited, let me explain that the Aramaic word for "mansion" we see in the Gospels is best translated as apartment. It's the name given to each new addition to the insula.

So the groom would be working away on his mansion, but he didn't even get to decide when it was done. He would work all day and sometimes at night, all the while waiting for his father's approval. The groom's father was the only one who had the privilege of deciding when it was done. I imagine those conversations went something like this.

"Come on, Dad!"

"Nope. You need a better door, son. You call that an entrance-way?"

The girl, meanwhile, would be waiting at her family home, keeping watch day and night, never knowing the day, the time, or the hour of her pending nuptials. Talk about excruciating. I can't imagine how my wife would have felt if she had to do all our wedding preparation without ever knowing what day it was going to happen.

Then, without any warning at all, the father would announce, "All right, son. It is finished. Go get your bride." The son would then rally his wedding party, in particular, his groomsmen. Together they would walk into the girl's town unannounced and blow their ram's horns, called *shofars,* and the man and his bride would run down the stairs and down the aisle.

Does any of this sound familiar?

Rewind the tape. Scholars believe that during the Passover feast, when Jesus got to the third cup—the cup of salvation—instead of laying it aside untouched as was the custom, He took it and drank it. It was His way of saying, "The coming Messiah? Yeah, He's here. It is I."

Then, even more unthinkably, Jesus held the cup before His disciples and in doing so was mysteriously and symbolically inquiring, "Will you marry Me?"

I can imagine the awkward moment that followed. The shuffling of feet, the furtive glances, someone blurting out, "Go for it, Peter! You're always rushing into things!"

And then they did. They drank. Perhaps they thought, *Well, we've followed Him this far. Let's see how far the rabbit hole goes.* Then Jesus laid it all out before them, essentially saying, "I'm gonna have to leave for a while. We won't see each other for this engagement time, but take heart. I'm sending My best man, the Holy Spirit, and He's going to communicate messages between you and Me. I'm going home to be with My Father, because in My

Father's insula are many mansions, and I'm going to prepare a place for you. While you wait for the wedding day, your name will be different. You will be called, One Who Was Bought with a Price. You will need to keep watch too. The day will come like a thief in the night, and even I don't know the day, the time, or the hour. The Father alone knows when the time will be, but when He decides, I'm going to come with My wedding party, the holy angels, and they're going to blow their heavenly shofars from the four corners of the earth, and I'm going to bring you home for the marriage supper of the Lamb."[2]

In light of this mystery, my world shakes.

We are more than His disciples.

We are more than His servants.

We are more than His friends.

We are more than His children.

We are His bride.

I know, some guys are reading this saying, "What? I ain't nobody's bride!" Relax, my man. It's an analogy. Christ uses the most intimate relationship to describe what He longs for from us. We, the church, are His bride. To top things off, we are often an unfaithful bride. Loved as we are, we, like Israel, constantly run away to pursue earthly pleasures and idols that are, in the end, lovers less wild.

And what does Christ do? He calls us back. Just as He commanded the prophet Hosea to marry an adulterous woman named Gomer. Not only did God call Hosea to marry Gomer, but He told him to go and rescue her after she sought out other lovers. Hosea was asked to bring her back, along with the children she had with other men. When I first read the book of Hosea, I started interrogating God on Hosea's behalf: "What's wrong with you, Lord! How dare You ask Your boy to do a thing like that! He was Your prophet, and You dragged his heart through the mud! Why on earth did You ask him to keep loving a woman who was so horrible to him?" When Hosea asked some of these very questions, God responded, "Go again, love a woman who is loved by another man and is an adulteress, even as the LORD loves the children of Israel, though they turn to other gods" (Hosea 3:1).

I can't help but wonder how different the divorce rate in the church would be if couples understood their relationship was meant to reflect God's covenantal love for His church. Our covenants to each other are not just about the rings and the ceremony but are meant to be a shining symbol to the world of how our God loves His bride, the church. That is why God says He hates divorce. It isn't because He wants to make divorced people feel bad. (He doesn't.) God hates divorce because it suggests to the world that He might one day break His vow with us. (He won't.) God hates divorce because, in effect, it paints an inaccurate picture of His love.

This is the relationship God longs to have with us. It is so much more than religion. It's so much more than mere rules and regulations. God's love for us is final and loyal and fierce. I've heard it said, "It's a far different thing to break a rule than it is to cheat on a lover." This thing is wild intimacy and an ever-longing invitation from the heart of a triune God who cannot help but love us. It is His nature. Of course, it will be a lifelong fight for us to rest in His love, because it is not in our human nature to love without reason. Yet God loves us without qualification. It pours out of Him like water from a spring. This divine relationship is what we were created for. So, follow the disciples' lead. Take and drink deeply. Let His yes to you evoke an ever-cascading yes *from* you. Let His love for you fill you to overflowing. Let His covenant bring you ever closer, ever onward, out of hiding, and into His arms.

15

Embrace the Cracks

Until the tears have left your eyes
Until the fear can sleep at night
Until the demons that you're scared of
 disappear inside
Until this guilt begins to crack
And the weight falls from your back
Oh, my dear, I'll keep you in my arms tonight.

—TENTH AVENUE NORTH, "OH MY DEAR"

A year before Kelly and I ever started talking about marriage, we had to have a talk to "air out the dirty laundry." This happens in every relationship (or it should). This is the time when the two of you decide whether you will be taking your relationship to the next level. I'm not sure what other people mean when they use this phrase, but I think "the next level" is slang for "actually being yourself." We had been dating for two years already, so we knew if matrimony was in our future, we would have to give each other a more complete picture of how our pasts had shaped who we had become. We told each other about past relationships, deep struggles, and all the missteps we wish we hadn't made along the way. We confessed the lines we wish we hadn't crossed and the mistakes we wish we could take back. There was one mistake in particular, though, that my wife refused to share.

"There is this one thing," Kelly started, "but I can't tell you. I promised I wouldn't tell anyone except my future husband." As you can imagine, I was insane with curiosity. I had to know. We talked late into the night. For nearly four hours in a motel stairwell, I begged and begged until I was finally able to drag it out of her. She told me something that she'd kept secret for far too long, and in a moment, it was like a curtain I couldn't even see before was lifted. It was like putting on glasses for the first time, when you're stunned at how blind you didn't know you were. Kelly took off the mask I didn't even know she was wearing, and I remember having to catch my breath at the beauty waiting underneath.

This conversation took place when we were both counselors for high school students at a winter ski retreat in West Virginia. We were actually at two different retreats, but at the same ski resort. My band was doing the music for one group at a hotel while Kelly was a counselor at another retreat happening down the road. It snowed heavily the entire weekend, but every night, I walked a mile in the snow (uphill both ways) to go sit outside her motel room door and talk. Despite the weather, I would not be thwarted.

On the third night of the retreat, we had our big relationship talk. Kelly had just begun to tell me her biggest, baddest secret, when she caught herself. "I can't tell you this. It's too terrible."

"Too terrible?" I gulped. Like yours, my head was whirring with all the greedy excitement of needing to know just how bad her past was. "What is too terrible?" I badgered her. "Did you assassinate someone? Did you drive a bus off a cliff? What did you do! You know you can't just stop like that! You're gonna have to tell me now!"

But that's when she went on to tell me this confession was reserved for no one but her husband, whoever that lucky man was going to be. Naturally, that sent me over the edge. I was relentless. I pleaded and pleaded until, several hours later, with mascara and tears running down her cheeks, Kelly finally broke. "All right. I'll tell you. But you'll never look at me the same way again."

She was right. I never looked at her the same after that. From that moment on, I loved her even more. I didn't realize this at the time, but the place where we have failed is exactly the place where we get to be loved. Seeing where she had screwed up gave me the chance to choose to love her. It didn't even feel like much of a choice, if I'm honest. The moment my future wife finally let me in and spoke her big, bad, dark secret, I seriously almost laughed in disbelief. "That's it?" I asked.

Her tiny streams of tears became rushing rivers. "What do you mean, 'that's it'?" she whimpered in between hysterics. For years, she had lived in a perpetual state of fear, and the floodgates finally opened when she simply brought it into the light. She couldn't believe how something that had become such a big deal to her could be such a small one to me.

It's worth reiterating that this is always how it is with God. No matter how big our mistakes are, they will always be small to Him. He's God. When you're the king of eternity, it's hard to be shocked. You've kind of seen it all. My wife was shocked by my reaction too. She couldn't believe that I was meeting her with acceptance, not judgment. To be clear, it wasn't even really acceptance. I was really sort of disappointed. I had been bracing myself for something much worse. When her admission came, it was a bit of a letdown. I mean, the way she worked it up you would have thought she was out on bail for a double homicide.

Now, I'm not saying, "Look at me! I'm awesome. I'm such a super spiritual guy! I see my wife through Jesus glasses." Hardly. I forget to see His way all the time. I just really couldn't believe she had been so hung up about something that, to me, really didn't seem so terrible. Of course, the opposite is true. Had she confessed to me and I overreacted, I could have given shame even more power than it already had over her. It's a sobering reality, isn't it? Our reactions have power and can help either undo chains or create new ones. When we confess to each other, our response can either feed shame's dark power or starve it.

Since that ski-retreat disclosure, I've gained new insight into James 5:16, which says, "Confess your sins to one another and pray for one another, that you may be healed." I had never really caught that last word before. Notice it doesn't say, "Confess your sins to one another, that you may be forgiven." We're forgiven when we come to God with our sins and receive His mercy. We are forgiven the moment we believe it. It's a done deal. But I truly believe some of us will never be healed in certain ways until we bring our secrets into the light.

What's the difference between healing and forgiveness? Healed from what? Well, confession ushers in healing from the belief that we have to save ourselves, for one thing. Our confession also invites God to heal the devastating effects of shame and condemnation. Instead of living a lie and wondering when we'll be found out, we can choose to confess and let God heal us. We can find healing for our nagging questions: *If I take my mask off, will they run? Do they love the real me, or do they only love the image I'm projecting?*

None of us can actually experience true acceptance until we let ourselves be fully known. When we hold our secrets back, praise from others falls flat because we know it isn't really us they're praising. It's the incomplete version. It's really the idea of us they love.

I truly believe confession can usher in healing from physical pain and sickness too. It's incredible what science has revealed about how bitterness and anxiety affect our physical bodies. I've read countless articles suggesting our bodies are a printout of our minds. Just the other day, a good friend of mine fainted on a golf course. He was rushed to the hospital, and the doctor said his body shut down from stress. Stress! What's happening in our hearts and minds influences our bodies. It doesn't take a doctor to know the instant improvement that would result if our minds were at peace. Now, if even our bodies are set free by truth, imagine how our souls benefit when we finally let the light in on our secrets.

Is That All You Got?

One thing I'm sure of: secrets will keep us from receiving the life of Jesus like nothing else can. From a worldly perspective, secrets seem to be worth keeping and shame can be a great motivator. Shame sometimes drives us forward to accomplish more. We may impress our friends, family, and colleagues alike, but more often than not, we'll also run ourselves into the ground. Without a deep knowledge that God knows us and loves us just as we are, many of us will try to work harder or perform more perfectly in an attempt to atone for all the ways we feel we've come up short. We may not realize that's what we're doing, but our constant fatigue and feelings of injustice give us away.

My friend Chuck says most of us know just enough about the Bible to feel really guilty. We know God is mad at us, that we're not good enough, and that we should all probably try a little harder. So we try and try until we fail one too many times. Then we throw in the towel. We never go deeper to find out just how redeemed we are. We haven't experienced lasting change because we haven't repented in awe of God's abounding kindness. We never experience the freedom of joyfully following Christ because we're too busy following Him for the justification He's already handed to us. Secrets keep us from finding out how redeemed we are. Shame and perfectionism keep us locked away. We stay hidden.

Why do we go on this way? Why do we stay in the shadows instead of walking in the light? Well, I think there are a million reasons, but I'll offer just a few. First, I think some of us are afraid to admit we need God to save us, because deep down we don't believe He will. What if Jesus isn't as merciful as some claim? What if we've out-sinned the grace of God? What if we reveal all our faults, only to see Jesus and our friends turn on us?

As silly as that sounds, I've thought that same thing. That's why I've tried to adopt my friend John's philosophy. John helps run a ministry in Arizona called Trueface, which is a church that operates the way AA does. He believes his number-one priority is to coax people out of their shame. John teaches everyone involved in the ministry that the only right and proper way to respond to someone's confession is with the short phrase "Is that all you got?" John reminds people that, after all, the blood of Jesus is stronger than the worst of our sin.

Here's some great news. You're actually worse than you think you are. As Timothy Keller wrote, "We are more sinful and flawed in ourselves than we ever dared believe, yet at the very same time we are more loved and accepted in Jesus Christ than we ever dared hope."[1] So take heart. Though you may feel humbled by your mistakes, you're not crushed by them. Yes, your sins sent Jesus to the cross, but He was glad to go to the cross for you. He didn't submit to death on the cross unwillingly but rather "for the joy set before him" (Hebrews 12:2, NIV). I'm convinced that Jesus is always running to us with open arms. He doesn't just love us when we're at our best because He joyfully died for us at our worst.

You don't need to worry about whether God will want to save you. I assure you, He does. And He already knows about the skeletons in your closet. His blood is enough to cleanse you of all sin, failure, or unrighteousness. It's like Clorox bleach for the soul. Knowing God will forgive you isn't always enough to motivate you to reveal to everyone else just how bad you've been, is it? In my life, it's not been doubting God's forgiveness that's kept me lip-locked but the knowledge that people won't share God's opinion on the matter. I've confessed things to plenty of people who didn't share my friend John's philosophy about confession. Instead of saying, "Is that all you got?" they winced and said, "Ooh, that's what you got."

My Porn Clock

A few years ago, I wrote a blog post titled "My Porn Clock." I explained that when we're on the road, I carry a small alarm clock into my bunk every night I spend on our tour bus. I do that so I won't even be tempted to bring my smartphone into my bunk with me, which would give me access to the entire internet, including porn. I leave my phone in a drawer in the front lounge of our bus. I take this precaution because I'm a man, and I know too many men who've been brought down by pornography addictions. So my porn clock is a means of keeping the guardrails up, so to speak. Do you know what happened when I published that blog entry? Scores of people wrote me and told me I must not be a Christian. At least ten people sent me angry messages proclaiming they would never listen to my music again. Mind you, I never even admitted to looking at porn. I didn't even say I wanted to look at it. The mere mention of guarding myself against it was enough to incur a mountain of shame.

Needless to say, I understand the concern of divulging too much. And even though a bunch of angry commenters piled humiliation on me, it was worth it. In the years since, I'd guess that more than a hundred men have walked up to me and told me privately that my blog post really spoke to them. Many of them said they felt supported and my vulnerability inspired them to get help for their own addiction. Despite any concerns about losing our sterling reputations, we have to remember we're not onstage in a Greek tragedy. The word *persona* stems from the Latin word for "mask." Actors would put on their personas before walking out onto the stages of those great amphitheaters of ancient Greece. Unlike them, some of us have never learned to take our masks off.

Let me ask you this. Aren't you tired of wondering whether the people in your life really love you? If you stay in hiding, you'll always wonder. The voices won't stop. *Do they really love me or the fake me? I want to take off my mask, but what if they only love me when I'm pretending! What will happen if I take it off?* Look. Don't you want to know what it would feel like to stop performing all the time? Isn't it exhausting? Wouldn't it be better to reveal your shame and your hang-ups and let the chips fall where they may? Maybe you'll lose a few friends, but wouldn't it be worth it? If they disappear, were they really your friends in the first place? At least then you'd know who your friends really are. You might even understand just what a masterpiece you are too.

We Are Stained-Glass Windowed Japanese Bowls

When I use the word *masterpiece,* I think of stained-glass windows and *kintsugi.* Kint-what? Exactly. We'll get to that. Let's start by thinking about stained-glass windows. You've seen those before. Take a good look at one next time you're passing by a church or cathedral. They're breathtaking. You might be asking, "Okay, but what's that got to do with me?" My friend Jon Guerra wrote a song called "Stained Glass." One of my favorite lines goes like this,

> We have stains, it's true
> but when your light shines through
> we all look like stained glass windows to you.[2]

I love that song so much. If you only focus in on one color, or stain, on an intricately crafted stained-glass window, you'll miss the glory of the overall design. All those cracks and stains come together to form a work of art when light shines through it. Up close, you only see a blemish, but if you stand back, you'll see the entire tiled tapestry.

Kintsugi is a Japanese art form that involves repairing broken pottery using lacquer dusted with gold or silver. This method creates something beautiful out of something broken and refuses to let cracks ruin a pot. Some would even argue that kintsugi pots become more beautiful through this process than they were at the start. No busted-up pot is beyond repair, and neither are we. The grace we give one another in moments of great weakness is like the gold poured into the cracks of the kintsugi pots. In his book *Scary Close,* Donald Miller wrote, "Grace only sticks to our imperfections."[3] And in the U2 song "Grace," which would go on to be the soundtrack of my wife's and my wedding video, Bono sings,

"Grace makes beauty out of ugly things." Grace finds beauty in ugly things. Do you know that in your heart? Do your friends? I sure hope so. I hope you know someone who understands the kind heart of Jesus enough that when you speak your secrets into the light, they speak the good news back to you, "Is that all you got?"

I know some of you are probably itching to know what it was Kelly did that was so terrible. Sorry, I'm not gonna tell you. Here's why. She married me, not you. The secrets she had certainly needed to be confessed, but not to everyone, not in public. This is a vital distinction. She confided in me, and that was enough. Confessing to me was enough to break the guilt that held her hostage for so many years. It even led her to share with a few other very important people in her life. Now that she has found healing, there is no need to revisit it. This is so important for us to understand. Confession isn't necessarily just for Instagram posts. I scroll through social media feeds and shake my head sometimes. Confessing to strangers isn't really the point, is it? It's not going to bring that healing you're after, I can tell you that. There is a huge difference between testifying to a timeline and humbly admitting my hang-ups to a friend. Jesus came to redeem us, but healing happens in community. Looking someone in the eye is part of the process. To look in the eyes of someone who cares for me, who may even be hurt by what I've done, but who is ready to forgive, that's where intimacy happens. There may even be ramifications for my sin or mistake. There will be pain and there will be consequences too. Sadly, not everyone is a safe place.

Having said that, I suppose it might do some of us good if all our sins were made public for everyone to see. Some of us might need that kind of push to force us out of our hiding places. There'd be nowhere else to go but to cling to Jesus our Savior if our mistakes were being broadcast on the five o'clock news. The point is, trust must be earned and, for many of us, practiced. However much grace you think someone needs, give them more. Remember, we're all doing life for the first time here. There's wide debate about who said it, but I love the quote, "Be kind. Everyone is fighting a hard battle." Indeed. Let's tread lightly on one another's hearts. Knowing this, we can bring our secrets into the light, one gospel-soaked experience at a time.

There aren't a whole lot of things I'm sure of, but the healing power of confession is one of them. I'm not kidding; it works every time. Maybe not as quickly as we'd like, but privacy is like oxygen for shame. When we open up the doors on the very worst things we've done, it's as if we're cutting off their air supply. Yes, it'll get messy, but it'll be worth it. I promise you.

Broken Foot / Healed Marriage

We met a couple who I'll call John and Lisa at a festival near Austin, Texas, a few years ago. They stood before us, beaming and holding hands. John told us how a year and a half earlier, he had been listening to our band's song "Oh My Dear" while cutting the grass. It just so happens that I wrote this song as a "confession story" about my wife and me.

"I was listening to it on my headphones," he said, "and God told me I needed to tell my wife I had been cheating on her." He shifted awkwardly before adding, "There had been multiple affairs, and I didn't think I'd ever be able to come clean. I came in from mowing, still sweaty and covered with grass. I took the headphones off and told her . . . She wasn't happy, of course. In fact, she broke her foot when I told her. She broke it kicking me in the shin as hard as she could."

She chuckled. "I did!"

At this point, our whole band was staring at them with mouths hanging open. "Well"—he paused briefly—"that was the beginning of a slow and arduous journey back together. We went to counseling, she forgave me, and eighteen months later, we've never been happier."

I still think about that couple and shake my head in disbelief. Not every story ends like that. Sadly, some of us come into the light and may have to face the consequences of our actions. We may not be met with the mercy we were hoping for.

Confession is always a risk, absolutely. But when we can let ourselves be completely known, we open up the potential to be completely loved, whatever the results. This usually follows on the heels of wild and risk-taking honesty. I know it's scary, but love doesn't fully grow between people who never fail. It grows in the cracks of our armor. As Leonard Cohen sang, "There is a crack in everything; that's how the light gets in."[4] Intimacy and connection blossom when we choose to love each other at our worst. Let's begin now. Disarm your guilt. Exposing our failures opens us up to being truly and deeply accepted as we are.

My wife has seen how love pours into the broken places. John and Lisa haven't been the only couple to tell me how "Oh My Dear" was an inciting force in moving them toward reconciliation.

Recently, a festival promoter in New Zealand told me how he had read the lyrics during a city council meeting going horribly wrong. He said the words pierced through the walls of hardness and helped shift the atmosphere in the room.

My wife shakes her head when I tell her these stories. "Never in a million years," she told me, "would I have ever imagined God would use my fear of confession in such poignant ways." Me neither. It's true, though. When we finally step into the light, we allow ourselves to be truly known, truly accepted, and truly used to help others find courage to do the same. The next time you think what you've done is too terrible for you to come clean, remember Jesus's blood is enough for all of us. We are Japanese jars of clay. We are stained-glass windows. We may be broken, but the repairs shape us into glowing testimonies to the power of what grace can do. Grace finds beauty everywhere, in everything. Friends, we have a Defender, so let's lay down our defensiveness. We have a Savior, so let's lay bare our secrets. It's time we were known in truth, not loved for our lies.

Chia Pet Spirituality

My wife is good at many things, but caring for houseplants is not one of them. Every month or so, I laugh as she wheels another load of shriveled foliage out to the waste bins by the side of our house.

"Why not get some plastic plants?" I suggest.

"I will have a green thumb," Kelly asserts, "if it's the last thing I do!"

"Look, babe. Maybe gardening isn't your thing. We all have

to accept our limitations in some areas. You're doing great with our children . . ."

She didn't like my assessments. Instead, she has prevailed. Do you know something? She's getting better. The plant in our bathroom has been alive for ten whole glorious months. I think we've turned a corner.

The reason plants are so hard to grow is that they're so particular. They have to have water, but not too much water. They need light, but not too much light. One of the things you quickly learn about houseplants is the difference between low-light and full-light plants. Most indoor plants are low-light plants. Don't make the mistake of trying to bring a full-light plant in your house; it's gonna die. Mark my words. Don't even try it. A full-light plant needs a lot of stinking light to thrive.

So do we.

Stick us in a dark room by ourselves, and we may limp along for a week or two, but eventually we're destined for a shriveled place next to the trash receptacles. We weren't made to stick it out alone in the shadows; we were made to live in the light. John 3:20–21 says, "Everyone who does wicked things hates the light and does not come to the light, lest his works should be exposed. But whoever does what is true comes to the light, so that it may be clearly seen that his works have been carried out in God."

We are made to live in the light. Jesus often spoke of His kingdom using agricultural terms such as seeds, trees, wheat, weeds, and harvest. This is beautiful and as relatable today as it was to His original audience. Without the aid of time-lapse photography, almost all plant growth is imperceptible. It's slow, painfully slow. If you've ever grown a garden, you know the thrill of seeing the first tiny shoot finally peeking its way through the dirt. You may also know the torture of staring at a green strawberry for weeks, waiting for the day it's ripe enough to pluck.

The last time my wife and I tried to grow strawberries, our dog gobbled up every last one of them before we could harvest them. We caught her red-handed (red-pawed, actually). Kelly had gone out the back door with an empty bowl, ready to feast on the sweet berries we'd been watching ripen for the last month. I heard her scream and went running outside to see her chasing our dog Blue around the backyard. Blue had jumped the garden fence and was carefully plucking each strawberry off, one by one. I didn't even know dogs liked fruit. Now I'm getting mad again just thinking about it. Strawberries are my favorite fruit. *Stinking dog!*

Spiritual growth can be as slow and maddening as gardening. Though I hate waiting as much as the next person, I love that Jesus accepts how slow our spiritual progress can be—plant-growing slow! Comparing our lives to gardening—such as the parable of the sower in Matthew 13—is His way of saying, "Relax. I know you feel like you're stuck in the same cycle, struggling with the same setbacks, but take heart. I'm working. You're growing. Even when you can't feel it. You're about to break through the dirt." As you know, God's not afraid to get His hands dirty. He welcomes our dirt. Jesus covered Himself in it, after all. He chased us all the way down into hell so we could be made clean. So what is left to be afraid of? We give each other our cracks and watch as gold and silver fill them in. God's grace is the water and the light. Before we know it, we'll find flowers growing through the cracks.

16

Bad Golf Is Good
for Your Heart

> Golf is the closest game to the game
> we call life. You get bad breaks from
> good shots; you get good breaks from
> bad shots, but you have to play the
> ball where it lies.
>
> —BOBBY JONES

Do you play golf? I started playing it about six years ago.
Before, I thought golf was just something you put on the
TV as the soundtrack to your Sunday nap. Now I've come
to believe it's the sport that most vividly helps us embrace our
mistakes, compose our minds, and move on after debilitating em-
barrassment. Some of my best friends in high school played, so I
tried to learn with them when I was sixteen. I went with them to

a driving range two or three times, but the whole thing felt so awkward that I gave it up quickly. Back then, I didn't understand the value of enjoying the process. I didn't like it when they said, "It's a game of misses." It was terribly unsatisfying. As a junior in high school, when I didn't get the hang of something quickly, I gave it up immediately. Golf was no exception. It didn't help that my friends were not the greatest instructors, so after several convoluted and conflicting suggestions on how to grip the club, I was certain this was not the sport for me. I mean, just holding the thing felt like hanging on to a wet spaghetti noodle with fish fins for hands. As I said, awkward. It didn't help when my buddy Nate concluded the lesson by zinging me in the middle of my back with a bladed sand wedge from fifty yards away. I hobbled to my car with a throbbing welt the size of a grapefruit and a deflated self-image. I vowed to never touch another golf club as long as I lived.

That resolve remained unchecked for well over a decade until Tenth Avenue North got the call to play a private house show for a fund-raising event. Due to my brief and unenjoyable interaction with golf, I was intimidated to learn that our host was a professional golfer. His name is Kevin, and since that first meeting, we've actually become great friends. We even host a charity golf tournament together now. However, things didn't start out so sweetly. When we met, Kevin wasn't aware of how grossly lacking in skills I was, so he recommended we all go out to TPC Scottsdale, a thirty-six-hole golf complex, to strike a few at the players' range. If you don't know what any of that means, don't worry. Neither did I. What I did know was I was severely underdressed in my torn jeans and T-shirt. "Tuck the shirts in, boys!" some older club members yelled out at us in the Arizona heat. "This ain't tennis!" I hadn't held a club in my hands since those few times in high school, so I could feel the hot beads of sweat sliding down my back as we walked onto the practice area.

I was awful too. Just awful. I think I almost killed three people. Members were glaring at me as I took chunk after chunk of pristine grass out of their meticulously groomed lawn. With every clumsy fruitless swing, I thought, *This must have been what Sisyphus felt.* But then a glorious moment came shattering through my humiliating toil. God looked down, beheld my futile labor, and decided to have pity upon my unskilled, wretched swinging. In an act of what could only be described as divine mercy, He allowed me to hit the sweet spot on the club and experience the ecstasy of the ball soaring effortlessly through the clouds and toward the range flag. I was no longer a disgrace. I was Tiger Woods. I whooped and hollered and did all the things you're not supposed to do on a golf course. I straddled the club and galloped around as if I were riding a pony. It was a magical moment.

The magic did not dissipate. Just the opposite. Rather, it escalated quickly into the erroneous belief that I was suddenly good at golf. Any golfers reading this are laughing to themselves, because you know how utterly impossible the sport is and how wickedly deceiving it is, all at the same time. It didn't help when Kevin sent some of us free golf clubs after we left. The following year, I became obsessed. I read books. I watched swing videos. I dreamed of my first hole in one and wondered how much work it would take to qualify for the PGA tour myself. I became, like most new amateurs, one more of golf's delusional victims. I was obsessed.

The worst part was I didn't actually get any better for a long time. In fact, it seemed like the better I became at hitting the ball, the worse my score was. Again, if you play golf, you know exactly what I mean. Now, just a few years after my first sweet strike of a golf ball, my fervor was rapidly waning. One bitter afternoon, it fizzled out completely.

I was out on a course with Jeff and Jason, the two guys in my band who grew up playing. They shared my love/hate relationship with the sport. So whenever we had a show near a decent course, we would throw our clubs on the bus and try to play a few holes the afternoon before our concert. One not-so-random day, I was having a particularly terrible time of things. It was raining and cold and I couldn't keep it together. I fell apart completely. The only thing worse than my swing was my attitude. I was throwing clubs down the fairways. I was screaming wildly at the squirrels who I was quite sure were laughing at me. If you've seen the movie *Happy Gilmore,* you have a good idea of how I was behaving. Jeff and Jason stopped looking me in the eye around the fifth hole. By the eighth hole, they asked me to get my own cart. At the end of the round, I slammed my clubs into the back of the van and sulked mightily. A few minutes into the cold, awkward ride back to the venue, Jeff leaned over to me and flatly stated, "You know, Mike, sometimes you're not any fun to play with at all." His candor changed my life.

My temper flared. My face reddened. I steadied my anger for a moment so I could properly unleash a tsunami of raging retort on him—but unexpectedly fell quiet. I wanted to scream, but the problem was I knew he was right. I had nothing to say. I was ashamed of myself. For the remaining fifteen minutes of the car ride, I had to do some serious soul searching. *What made me so mad? Why was I so stinking competitive? Why did my golf score threaten my worth so deeply? How could a sport bring me so much anguish?*

Perhaps you think I was really overthinking all this, but I don't think I was. It's often the little things that reveal the greatest truths. That day, cold, wet, and humiliated, I realized something. God was way less interested in me playing good golf and was much more interested in me playing bad golf well. Anyone can feel great about themselves when everything is on a perfect trajectory. But that doesn't help us when things come unglued. I don't know about you, but I don't want to be a good golfer only when I'm doing great. I want to be a good golfer when I've just shanked one into the lake. It's all about attitude. That's what God is after, right? It's not like I could beat Jesus at golf, anyway. He wants to rule in our hearts, souls, and minds, way before we rule on the scorecard. My golf score will ebb and flow, but that doesn't mean my joy has to. I want to stay in tune with my heart so I'm ready for the next shot, even if it's from the woods. I don't want to overcome failures. I want to embrace them.

Let me add one more thing here, because I know some of you are reading the word *golf* the same way my dad watches it: asleep. Did you know that the greatest shots in golf history have come almost exclusively on the tails of the absolute worst shots? Bubba Watson hit out of the straw to win the Masters in 2012, after he hooked his drive and was stuck behind the trees.[1] Jordan Spieth hit an unbelievable blind approach shot from behind a TV tower to come from behind and win the British Open in 2017. His previous drive was probably a hundred yards in the wrong direction.[2] Tiger Woods won too many to count from unthinkable situations, leaving the crowd shaking their heads in disbelief and wondering, "How did he hit that from *there*?" The greatest opportunities often come on the backs of terrible mistakes. In this way, golf is one of my favorite metaphors for life. We have no control over changing our mistakes. What's done is done. The drive is out of bounds, and it's not coming back. But if we're not in the clubhouse, then we're still playing. We can wallow in regret, or we can play it as it lies. In this sense, golf has freed me up to enjoy my life more, however I'm scoring. Kevin told us his mom has taught him how to enjoy the game like no one else. She'll take twelve putts to close out a hole, but once the twelfth putt falls, she pumps her fist like she's won a tour event.

I want to be like Kevin's mom. I want to pump my fist in the face of both victory and defeat. After all, if my scorecard already reads "Redeemed," then I'm freed up to take as many mulligans as I need to hit one pure. Even my wayward swings become opportunities for something truly miraculous. Every shot sets up another chance to get it right, regardless of what just went wrong. This is how God's life changes my will. Yes, I'd love to shoot under par, but I'd much rather enjoy the time I'm out there. Yes, I know you'd love to accomplish a ton with your life, but how you go about it is even more important. The best news is that we get to keep on swinging. As Ben Hogan once said, "The most important shot in golf is the next one."

Bad Sets and Summer Storms

While God was using golf to teach me about bad shots, He was using a band called Hawk Nelson to teach me how to handle musical miscues gracefully. The lead singer, Jon, has one of the most beautiful attitudes of anyone I've met in the music industry. He does music the way I want to play golf. He keeps looking for the next little miracle, no matter how bleak the moment gets. We were out on tour together when one night the inevitable happened. Hawk was halfway through their set when all their instruments inexplicably shorted out. The front-of-house speakers started cutting out, and to top it off, their computer onstage crashed. The band limped along through the rest of the set in disjointedly dismal fashion. I could see the expressions sweeping over his bandmates' faces as Jon rushed by me to start tearing down their gear once the travesty of a set had concluded. I could tell he was pretty bummed about the way things had gone. I gave him a few minutes to cool down before hunting him down to offer my condolences. To my surprise, I found him backstage, rolling cables and laughing with the drummer about the train wreck that had just transpired.

I asked him, "How are you keeping such a good attitude right now?" His response? "Well . . ." He looked down at the floor while methodically spooling cable over his arm until the right words came. "I just thought, anyone can play music when everything works perfectly. It's when things go wrong we get the chance to be professionals." I love this response. When things go wrong, we get an opportunity we never would have had otherwise. I want to live my life like that.

Playing concerts for a living has definitely reinforced this belief over the years. A set rarely ever goes exactly as you hoped. If you can't learn to roll with the punches, live performance probably isn't going to be your cup of tea. I can't even tell you how many times I've changed the set list at the last minute, and it completely backfired. I'll get this feeling down in my bones that we're supposed to do a particular song we haven't played in five years. Mid-set, I'll call it out to the band, and they'll look back at me in utter terror. Our lighting guy will be staring wide eyed out in the audience. I can see him whispering to our soundman, "What song IS THIS?" Sure enough, I'll take the risk, call it out, and we'll stumble through it, everyone unanimously agreeing after the show, "Well, that was a bad move!" But every once in a while, something happens. Not every time mind you, maybe not even one time out of ten. But one time in a hundred maybe, someone in the crowd will tell me after the show that the song I threw in was the song God used to change their life. They felt it was His love letter to them in a season of devastation. They'll say, "I can't believe you played it. I felt like God was telling me I matter to Him." I'll beam, and the rest of the band will groan. Despite the musical devastation my spontaneity unleashed, one testimony will validate me to keep on trying. Again, it's probably a 1 percent return rate, which doesn't seem like a good move. But I can't help but feel it's worth it. Jesus did say something about leaving the ninety-nine to find the lost one, didn't He? (Matthew 18:12.) I like the idea that God may actually call me to try things that have no point other than to remind me I'm not the greatest. I don't have to be perfect, and I'm not as cool as I'd like to think I am. He's only asking me to listen to Him, risk greatly, and be ready to laugh at myself.

Last summer in Chippewa Falls, I had to laugh as I watched my set list literally blow off the stage and into the Wisconsin night. After our sixth song, an absurdly isolated thunderstorm materialized out of nowhere. A large full moon had just risen in the summer sky, and I was too busy admiring it to notice the impending apocalypse forming above us. I even encouraged the audience, "Look at that moon, everybody! It's gonna be an amazing night!" Two minutes later, with clear skies in every other direction, a mighty thunderstorm cell formed directly overhead. Another thirty seconds passed, and the entire crowd was running for cover amid unimaginable winds and torrential downpour.

The full moon seemed to be laughing at us, hanging lazy and unflinching. Meanwhile, pandemonium unleashed above us. The storm only lasted fifteen minutes or so, but it was enough to knock out the soundboard, the light board, and any other board with electricity running through it. The show was over. My friend Mandisa had performed just before us, and she was still sitting side stage. I asked her why she wasn't seeking shelter on her bus, and she quickly responded that she was forlorn because she had been waiting for us to sing her favorite song. If you know her, you know she's the greatest celebrator of other artists. We joked that if she wasn't performing, she'd be front row with every artist's T-shirt on. After every act, she'd pull the top T-shirt off to reveal the next band's name. I felt so encouraged, I picked up my dripping guitar and sang a hurried chorus with her back by the gear cases.

Mandisa gave me a jovial high five as the photographer for the festival ran up to inform us we never played her favorite song either. So I sang one more, but by this time, a small crowd had regathered at the front of the stage. The downpour had decreased to an intermittent spittle. I ran out to meet them. I kept singing. The people who hadn't run for their cars began to come out of hiding from underneath the grandstands. Suddenly there were a few hundred of us, standing in the mud, clothes soaked through, spirits soaring.

Again, I'm not trying to paint some hero portrait of myself here. I've just learned from past mistakes. I could have marched off the stage to pout once the storm started. I've done that before. I could have glowered angrily because the whole night had been ruined and there was no point in going forward. I've done that before. I could have missed out. I could have missed what ended up being a much sweeter moment than any that could have happened had the whole night gone exactly according to plan. But I didn't this time. This time I remembered to play the next shot, whatever it looked like. I remembered what life looks like when we let Christ be our life. It looks like playing bad golf well and joyfully stumbling through bad set lists. We can let go of how things were meant to go, and we can embrace what is. To me it seems golf and concerts keep trying to tell us to play it as it lies. It's incredible to find that what's usually keeping us from joy isn't our circumstances but rather our death grip on how our circumstances should have gone differently.

How would things change for you if fear of failure were no longer a factor? You will fail; you won't be perfect; you'll end up in the sand or in the trees or in the middle of a storm. But maybe that's part of learning to follow the way of grace. For me, it's really freeing to know failure is part of success. If you view failure as a hiccup on the road to what really matters, you can let God's life invade your will. Remember that He's after your heart. Failure is just as important as success, because we usually learn much more about our value and identity when we fail than when we succeed.

17

I Still Don't Know What I'm Doing (Maybe I'm Not Supposed To)

The place God calls you to is the place where your deep gladness and the world's deep hunger meet.

—FREDERICK BUECHNER, *WISHFUL THINKING*

've been asked more than once, "When did you know this was God's will for your life? When did you know He called you to be a musician?"

My answer? "He didn't, and I don't." This isn't usually a helpful response. I've seen many eager young musicians severely disappointed. Their faces will contort. Trying to get a grasp of what I'm saying, they'll ask, "Well, what about Chris Tomlin? You've toured with him, right? What's his secret?"

I have to tell the truth. "Bro, I hate to break it to you. He doesn't know what he's doing either. We're all guessing, my man. Besides, being a musician isn't God's call on our lives. He didn't call me or Chris Tomlin or anyone else to this. He called us to go into all the world and make disciples."

The conversation usually deteriorates from there. Most of the kids drilling me with those sorts of questions aren't looking for heart advice. They're looking for practical tools to get to the top. I can't blame them. I was in the same headspace years ago. I had randomly become friends with a pair of Texan gentlemen who went by the artist name Shane & Shane. I guess I should say they *go* by that name. They're still alive. The Shanes had just played at my college's spiritual pep rally week, and I remember grilling them with my own music business questions.

Shane Everett, the sassy Shane, was up to his shoulders in engine grease, working on their tour bus. I had found him under the bus after their concert, and I was in rapid-fire delivery mode, peppering him with questions: "How did you get a record deal?" "Where did you record?" "What was the next step you took after you wrote your songs?"

I can't remember exactly what Shane said in response to me, but I remember it was something to the effect of "Just keep singing, man. If God wants you to do it, doors will open. If He doesn't, they'll close."

I remember hating this answer. I wanted to shout, *Don't mess with me. Give me the secrets, Shane! I know you have them!* I stewed silently as I handed him a wrench. I could never have known I'd be giving the same advice fifteen years later.

Truth is, I still don't know what I'm doing, and maybe, as Shane implied, I'm not supposed to. That's really hard to remember. God's Word is a lamp unto our feet (Psalm 119:105), not a floodlight for our interstate. God calls us into a life of faith because He wants us close. I've read that the "green pastures" mentioned in Psalm 23 were actually little tufts of grass growing overnight in the Israeli desert outside Jerusalem. When David wrote that God would make him lie down in green pastures, he was referring to the shepherds who led their sheep out into the wilderness, looking for just enough grass to make it to the next meal. This is so different from the pictures in my childhood Bible. They had the sheep reclining on green lawns like a bunch of French teenagers. Sporting sunglasses and playing volleyball, the sheep in my Bible were living that resort life. According to my studies, though, David had something else in mind. In Psalm 23, God isn't offering us luxurious provision; He's offering us abundant life . . . sustenance. He's calling us to intimate fearlessness and absolute dependence. He wants us to be His, and He wants us to act as though we believe it. If we had certainty about our lives and our futures, what need would we have for His presence? God gives us a blueprint for our hearts, not the keys of success for our profession.

I first heard the David Wilcox song "Hold It Up to the Light" a few years before talking to Shane under the bus. I was on a long road trip, heading back home from college. Fredericksburg was a fourteen-hour drive from West Palm Beach. I would get on Interstate 95 and take it the whole way. A friend had recommended

Wilcox's *Live Songs and Stories* album to me, and this one song changed how I viewed decision-making forever. The bridge exclaims in prayerful inquisition, "But I see if you gave me a vision, would I never have reason to use my faith?"[1] This one refrain was enough for me to believe God may never fill me in on His whole plan. If He did, I wouldn't ever get to use my faith. Hebrews 11:6 bolsters my conclusions: "Without faith it is impossible to please God" (NIV).

If God truly does own the whole world and everything in it, then I have to believe promotion and opportunity are His as well. This frees me up to adopt the singular mandate from Jesus in Matthew 28:18–20 as my mantra. I'm not a musician. I'm not an artist or an author or any other impressive label I can think up for my bio. I'm a "discipler." I make disciples. I may not know what I'm doing for a paycheck, but I know whom I'm helping with the paycheck I got.

Now, making disciples has been confused with a great many other things. It's been confused with missions, evangelism, and pastoring, to name a few. I don't think it means you have to pack your bags and move to Africa unless your heart burns for that continent. (If it does, then by all means go). But that's not what making disciples means. At least, not what I've gathered through studying the Bible. I take Jesus's command "Go and make disciples" to mean "Go walk with people. Wherever you are, whatever you're doing, be available to the people in your life. Walk with them step by step, until they begin to see how much I love them and learn how to remain in Me." This is rarely sexy. Prestige is easier than patronage. But Jesus loves it when we learn the wasteful ways of the kingdom.

Where Passion and Provision Collide

Jesus's one irrefutable law of being His disciple was, "Whoever abides in me and I in him, he it is that bears much fruit" (John 15:5). That's it. "Abide." Yep. So annoying. If you're like me, you were probably hoping for something other than intimacy with Jesus to solve all your problems, but He's not going to heal you any other way. The only thing required, and the only thing that works, is to be with Him. Only from that place, from that deep soul understanding, can we begin to bless the world.

In 2 Corinthians 5:17–18, Paul helps me understand how my calling to make disciples spills over from my calling to abide in Jesus: "Therefore, if anyone is in Christ, he is a new creation. . . . All this is from God, who through Christ reconciled us to himself and gave us the ministry of reconciliation." He introduces a provocative word, *reconciliation.*

Roll that word around for a bit. Is reconciling the big call you dreamed of having? It's such a perplexing way to describe our purpose, don't you think? Of all the words Paul could have used, he chose *reconciliation.* Essentially, he's saying, "You exist on this planet to forgive people and convince them they're forgiven. That's your job here." You think your ministry is music? Nope. It's reconciliation. You think your ministry is leadership? Nope. Reconciliation. Business? Pastoring? Missions? Architecture? Plumbing?

Teaching? The list goes on. Whatever you feel you've been called to do, I can assure you that the primary reason you're here is to reconcile.

What exactly does *reconcile* mean? *To make peace.* What better way to describe our purpose on earth? We're here to use our talents in such a way that they help others find peace with God and peace with one another. We are here to build bridges, not burn them down.

I pray in some small way my ramblings might unlock a new understanding for you. I pray God might pry your fingers off your plan for your life, and instead you would be ready to receive more of His life for your plan. I pray you would find new purpose for doing what you love. I don't think I'll ever find a better litmus test for my calling than Frederick Buechner's advice in his book *Wishful Thinking,* "The place God calls you to is the place where your deep gladness and the world's deep hunger meet."[2]

Find out what makes you come alive, and go do that thing, but not for yourself alone. Remember, God is "for us" in that He frees us to become "for Him." Don't just go do things that make you pumped about yourself. You won't get happy that way, anyway. Go figure out what you love, and then figure out how to make other people happy doing it. That's the sweet spot. Do the things that make you come alive in a way that meets the world's great needs. Like weavers reweaving a blanket in the places it's worn through, we are here to reweave the world. We are here as ambassadors of redemption. We are here to reconcile it.

Don't just ask what the world needs, either. If you approach serving in that way, you'll only burn yourself out, and God gets no glory from that. We must keep asking these questions: *What is my deep gladness, and what is the world's great hunger? Where do those two things collide?* This is the goal. This is how the kingdom comes through each of our lives, one breath at a time.

Some of us ask ourselves what the world needs, and then we put our heads down and work away. "This is what God wants of me," we say. We schlep through life doing what we know God wants, while bitterness creeps into our hearts when we're not recognized in the ways we feel we should be or we're not given the honor we think we deserve. We slowly begin to feel like the prodigal son's older brother. "Here I am! Slaving away for You! Where is my fatted calf?"

On the other side, some of us go the way of the prodigal. "Okay! What makes me feel good? I'm no use unless I'm happy, so I need to 'just do me' right now." Saint Irenaeus of Lyons is quoted as saying, "The glory of God is man fully alive,"[3] right? But this mentality has to be held in check. "Feeling alive" can easily be a blanket statement to justify our selfishness. The prodigal wasn't happy in the slop. Mystically, in the kingdom of God, to be fully alive is to first fully die. If we go for the passion of the self-fulfilled life only, we may find ourselves quite far from the sort of life God intends.

If Jesus went to the cross for the joy set before Him, then we ought to serve the world for joy. Serve *for* joy. We don't serve just to serve, and we don't try to get joy for joy's sake either. We are called to make disciples, so how do we do that in a way that serves them, while filling our hearts? This is what I end up telling people when they ask me how I became a musician. I simply respond,

"No, God didn't call me to music necessarily, but He did wire me with unique abilities and a love for songwriting and people. So now I'm just trying to do this in a way that helps make disciples."

I wish I did a better job of remembering this. I wish the church did a better job of teaching people that we can follow God's call in a million different occupations. Martin Luther once said, "God is milking the cows through the vocation of the milk-maid."[4] What he meant was that every job is holy, if the one doing the job does it to the glory of God. Simply doing the thing you were uniquely wired to do, to bring glory to the One who made you to do it, is essentially your calling.

Ephesians 2:10 says, "For we are his workmanship, created in Christ Jesus for good works, which God prepared beforehand, that we should walk in them." The New Living Translation says we are His "masterpiece." The Greek word is *poema,* from which we derive our English word *poem.* We are a well-crafted, one-of-a-kind love song written by God. We are stained-glass windowed Japanese bowls. This is phenomenal news. It's not up to you and me to find, or even create, the good works God has for us to do. We must simply walk in them. Be the poem God has already written. For me, this is a game changer. When I wake up, I need to simply ask myself, *All right, self, what things do we think God has created for us today? Let's keep our eyes open, lest we miss the joy He's got in store.* I no longer am wondering if I obeyed perfectly or if I somehow ruined the plan. I just keep saying yes. Like I said before, I simply get up and live the perpetual yes in His continual presence.

God Is Not a Pirate

Every day I have to convince myself God is not a pirate. Maybe I watched *Goonies* one too many times as a kid, but I've spent most of my life thinking He's keeping the way I should go a secret. He isn't. He isn't hiding His will for me on some cosmic treasure map. He isn't chuckling to Himself, wondering whether or not I'm going to navigate the booby traps, stay on course, or end up another flattened Chester Copperpot. God's not a pirate; He's the treasure.

A few summers ago, my friend Jon and I were sitting by a lake in western Canada, overlooking the mountains of Alberta. Gorgeous. We were there to play a festival nearby. A couple of us had spent the day wandering the river, and a few even stripped down to their underwear and jumped into the icy water. In the late afternoon, we found ourselves pontificating, and Jon said to me, "I feel like our lives are a lot like nature. God made the river, the lake, the mountains, the forest, and then He said, 'Well, what do you want to do? You want to climb the bank? Cool. You want to jump in? Go right ahead!' Maybe God wanted our lives to be like one of those 'choose your own adventure' books from my childhood. The ending is secure, so get out there and see what happens."

I couldn't help but feel my heart start racing. "No, no, no. I don't want to have to make a choice. I don't want to wander! Give me the instruction manual, God! Give me some parameters!"

Well, He does, but not the way I want Him too. He says to be joyful and pray continually and that sort of thing. God doesn't so much tell us what to do with our lives as tell us how to live them. And it's not by making a ton of money or becoming a great leader or person of influence. It's more about how to surrender every moment to trust God is who He says He is and that He loves you.

The Best Is Yet to Come

So now what? I don't know. Yes, that's right. You just read this entire book just to have me tell you I don't know what things God has created for you to walk in every morning. I know a few things from Micah 6:8. He wants you to walk with Him. He wants you to be humble. He wants you to carry yourself fairly and justly. He wants you to love mercy. That much I know. But I don't know what He has uniquely crafted you to do. I don't know what good works He has created in advance for you.[5] Here's the secret, though: nobody else knows either. So many books and conferences are advertised and sold in an attempt to usurp the role of the Holy Spirit, but don't buy in. No one else can be the Holy Spirit. If God's desire is closeness with you more than what you can produce, then it would make sense for Him to say something like, *No one else but My Spirit can give you answers like that. I want you coming to Me with those questions, because I want you!* Our Father still longs to walk with us on the journey, just as He walked with Adam and Eve in the cool of the day. This, I believe, is what Paul is getting at when he writes in Galatians 5:16, "Walk by the Spirit, and you will not gratify the desires of the flesh."

I'll raise one last question, and it may seem a bit strange. Are you worried Jesus will come back too soon? I know that's a weird question to end a book with, but be real with yourself for a second. What are you looking forward to so much that it would actually be quite a disappointment if God came back before it happened? Maybe it's a job promotion. Maybe it's a birthday. We joke, but maybe it's getting married or having sex. What if Jesus comes back too soon? Is it possible that whatever thing you're looking forward to more than Him is actually threatening to become your life?

You might be saying, "Come on, Mike, don't be such a buzz-kill. Don't end the book that way!"

Look, I say all that to say, what if you've hedged your bets on something that will eventually be taken away? What if you already had all the life and all the joy and all the peace you'll ever need, and it's being offered to you right now? Not only that, but what if the best is always yet to come? First Peter 1:3–4 says, "He has caused us to be born again to a living hope . . . to an inheritance that is imperishable, undefiled, and unfading, kept in heaven for you."

As C. S. Lewis said, "There are better things ahead than any we leave behind."[6] In every season, at any time, every single day of our lives, the best is always yet to come. In every question and every heartache, the best is yet to come. In every triumph and every tragedy, the best is yet to come. Let's release our stranglehold on our lives and our wills and all the ways we've dreamed of seeing our lives going. Let's give up on finding some secret will for our lives. In fact, let's let our lives go. Surrender. Keep surrendering. Let His life come rushing in. Let it swallow up all our ideas and all our dreams and all our grand plans for success. Keep our hands open to change and our hearts open to heavenly invasion. In the end, it's not our story, anyway. It's His. And I don't know about you, but I've read the ending. And nothing changes our present reality like what we believe about our future.

Notes

**If This Book Were to Have an Introduction,
This Would Be It**

1. Brennan Manning, *Ruthless Trust: The Ragamuffin's Path to God* (New York: HarperCollins, 2000), 5.
2. Cyndi Lauper and Rob Hyman, "Time After Time," *She's So Unusual*, Columbia Records, 1983.

Chapter 1: Jordan River or Red Sea?

1. David Wilcox, "Hold It Up to the Light," *Live Songs & Stories*, What Are Records?, 2002.
2. Deuteronomy 31:8, NIV.
3. Romans 8:28.
4. Exodus 14:8–31.
5. Joshua 3:6–17.

Chapter 2: 42 Trips to the Principal's Office

1. In reference to the scene in *Dead Poets Society* when the character Todd Anderson stands up on his desk and says "O Captain! My Captain!" See www.imdb.com/title/tt0097165/quotes/?tab=qt&ref_=tt_trv_qu.
2. Tenth Avenue North, "You Are More," *The Light Meets the Dark*, Reunion, 2010.

Chapter 4: Dreams Change (and That's Okay)

1. "Tangled: Quotes," www.imdb.com/title/tt0398286/quotes/?tab=qt&ref_=tt_trv_qu.

2. C. S. Lewis, *Mere Christianity* (New York: HarperOne, 2001), 123.

3. Daniel Schorn, "Transcript: Tom Brady, Part 3," *60 Minutes,* November 4, 2005, www.cbsnews.com/news/transcript-Tom -Brady-part-3.

4. Dietrich Bonhoeffer, "Notable Quotes," The Dietrich Bon- hoeffer Institute, http://tdbi.org/dietrich-bonhoeffer/notable -quotes.

5. Francis Chan, "Follow Jesus," January 16, 2012, Basic Series from David C Cook, video, 1:16, www.youtube.com/watch ?v=K7UIPx9-jqc.

6. Malcolm Gladwell, *David and Goliath: Underdogs, Misfits, and the Art of Battling Giants* (New York: Back Bay Books, 2015), 49–50.

Chapter 5: Capitalistic Christianity

1. Ben Rector, "The Men That Drive Me Places," *Brand New,* Aptly Named Recordings, 2015, https://www.youtube.com /watch?v=-OlpwJOsMgU.

2. Dietrich Bonhoeffer, *Letters and Papers from Prison* (New York: Touchstone, 1997), 10.

3. "Glossary: In Curvatus in Se," *Mockingbird,* www.mbird .com/glossary/incurvatus-in-se.

Chapter 6: The Ministry of Interruption

1. Matthew 25:40, NIV.

2. Mother Teresa, *In the Heart of the World: Thoughts, Stories, and Prayers* (Novato, CA: New World Library, 1997), 17.

3. This is a paraphrase often attributed to Mother Teresa, but she was not recorded saying these exact words. See www.mother teresa.org/08_info/Quotesf.html.

4. Although this quotation is often attributed to Winston Churchill, according to the International Churchill Society, he did not say it. More information at https://winstonchurchill .org/resources/quotes/quotes-falsely-attributed.

Chapter 7: The Leader Label Lie

1. Note that the Greek word for *Peter* means "rock."

2. *Dapper* is a late Middle English word, probably originating from a Middle Low German or Middle Dutch word, meaning "strong" or "stout" (https://en.oxforddictionaries.com /definition/dapper). The original thirteenth-century meaning of *heartburn* was "lust" (www.vocabulary.com/dictionary /heartburn). Inmates weren't understood to be people occupying prisons or mental hospitals until the latter half of the nineteenth century (english.stackexchange.com/questions /116001/how-did-inmate-evolve-to-only-apply-to-prisons-and -asylums). In the late sixteenth century, *bully* described a person who was "admirable, gallant, or jolly" (en.oxford dictionaries.com/definition/bully). *Balderdash* originally meant "a senseless mixture of liquids, as of milk and ale" (www .collinsdictionary.com/us/dictionary/english/balderdash). Used to describe a plant that produced other plants, *matrix* also meant a breeding animal (www.merriam-webster.com /dictionary/matrix). See also www.news.com.au/lifestyle /health/words-that-dont-mean-what-they-used-to/news -story/51201579cef4489251792042ac0a5880.

3. Mike Lotzer, "Common vs. True Virtue," Faith Covenant Church, August 7, 2014, http://faithcovenant.org/common -vs-true-virtue. Jonathan Edwards's original treatise on this topic, *The Nature of True Virtue,* can be found at http:// edwards.yale.edu/archive?path=aHR0cDovL2Vkd2FyZHMue

WFsZS5lZHUvY2dpLWJpbi9uZXdwaGlssby9nZXRvYmp
lY3QucGw/Yy43OjYud2plbw==.

4. Brent Gambrell, *Living for Another: More of Others, Less of You* (Nashville: Abingdon, 2017), 134–35.

Chapter 8: The Naked Marine

1. This idea appears in the gospels of Matthew, Mark, and Luke. See Matthew 16:24–26.
2. Louie Giglio, *I Am Not but I Know I Am: Welcome to the Story of God* (Colorado Springs: Multnomah, 2012), 92.
3. Eugene H. Peterson, *First and Second Samuel* (Louisville, KY: Westminster John Knox Press, 1999), 3.
4. *Dan in Real Life,* directed by Peter Hedges, Touchstone Pictures, 2007.
5. Rick Warren, *The Purpose Driven Life* (Grand Rapids, MI: Zondervan, 2002), 148.
6. John 13:34–35.
7. John 13:23; 19:26; 20:2; and 21:7, 20.
8. Matthew 6:3.
9. Matthew 11:30.
10. Timothy Keller, *The Freedom of Self-Forgetfulness: The Path to True Christian Joy* (Youngstown, OH: 10Publishing, 2012).

Chapter 10: I Stopped Asking God to Use Me

1. Psalm 50:9–11.
2. John 8:54, 13:31–32; Romans 15:5–6.

Chapter 11: Wasting Time on God

1. ACTS stands for Adoration, Confession, Thanksgiving, and Supplication.

2. Dallas Willard, *The Great Omission: Reclaiming Jesus's Essential Teachings on Discipleship* (New York: HarperCollins, 2006), 61.

3. Brennan Manning, *Abba's Child: The Cry of the Heart for Intimate Belonging* (Colorado Springs: NavPress, 2015).

4. Aaron Weiss, "A Glass Can Only Spill What It Contains," *Brother, Sister,* Capitol Christian Music Group, 2006.

5. Henry Scougal, *The Life of God in the Soul of Man* (Jersey City, NJ: Start Publishing, 2012).

6. Joseph Hart, "Come Ye Sinners," 1759, public domain.

7. Henri J. M. Nouwen, *Gracias!: A Latin American Journal* (Maryknoll, NY: Orbis Books, 1993), 69–70.

Chapter 12: Always Available Joy

1. *Inside Out,* directed by Peter Doctor, Pixar Animation, 2015. The scene of Sadness helping Riley can be viewed at www.youtube.com/watch?v=ISaHt3ps1dM.

2. Jars of Clay, "The Valley Song (Sing of Your Mercy)," *Furthermore,* Essential, 2003.

3. Matthew D. Hammitt et al., "Whatever You're Doing (Something Heavenly)," *We Need Each Other,* Sparrow Records, 2008.

4. Todd White, "When Healing Does Not Come," June 17, 2014, video, 19:56, www.youtube.com/watch?v=ppOLPHwDgZc.

5. A. W. Tozer, *The Pursuit of God* (Harrisburg, PA: Christian Publications, 2015), 11.

6. According to Jewish tradition, the soul hovers over the body for three days before departing this world. More information can be found at https://reformjudaism.org/glimpses-afterlife.

7. Fyodor Dostoyevsky, *The Brothers Karamazov* (Mineola, NY: Dover, 2005), 213.